INTRODUCTION

As every teacher of typewriting knows, a student's typing rate, speed and accuracy can vary from week to week or even from day to day. There are many reasons for the fluctuations but one of the important factors is the difficulty of the copy material being used. It is not easy for students and teachers to determine the progress that is being made when the straight-copy materials being used to measure progress vary in their degree of difficulty.

Research studies have strongly recommended that the following factors should be controlled if the material is to have validity for measurement: the stroke intensity, the syllabic intensity, and the occurrence of high-frequency words. The nature of the material used in this book made it difficult to control the percentage of high-frequency words; however, considerable care was taken to control both the stroke and syllabic intensity of the writings. The stroke intensity ranges from 5.48 to 5.58 with a mean of 5.54, and the syllabic intensity ranges from 1.36 to 1.44 with a mean of 1.40.

This book also contains drills, graduated speed and accuracy sentences, and graduated skill-building paragraphs which may be used to develop speed and accuracy, either separately or concurrently, at the one- and two-minute level.

Drills

Any activity which demands concentrated physical and mental effort requires a short, intense period of preparation, a warm-up, which will enable the participant to perform at his highest level. Typists must prepare themselves by developing their powers of concentration and by practising proper muscular control of their fingers. Drills fulfil this function admirably, first because their nonsensical character requires great mental concentration and, secondly, because their simplicity encourages smooth, continuous stroking.

Only three or four minutes should be spent "warming up" the fingers. Students should start very slowly and gradually increase their rates until they are typing as quickly as they can with a smooth, continuous rhythm. If a rhythm pattern is broken by going too quickly, the student concerned should slow down, then gradually work upwards once again.

If students are having trouble with a particular drill, if their stroking is uneven or their rhythm ragged, they should be encouraged to repeat the drill as often as is necessary to master it.

Speed and Accuracy Sentences

The speed and accuracy sentences were included in this book for the purpose of short intensive timings, and they may be used in two different ways:

1. The speed and accuracy sentences are both arranged in one-word increments (5 strokes) from ten to twenty-five words, so that students may move up the ladder one word at a time.

2. The speed and accuracy sentences are also arranged with three sentences at each level with the stroke and syllabic intensity ranging from low, the easiest,

Skill-Building Paragraphs

The skill-building paragraphs are graduated in two-word increments and were designed for one-minute timings; however, there is no reason why the paragraphs cannot be used for two-minute timings, by having the students repeat the same paragraph twice, for purposeful repetition is a valid tool in building skill.

The skill-building paragraphs may be used in two ways: for building speed or for developing skill (speed and accuracy concurrently). If a student's goal is to increase speed, then advancement should be permitted with a fairly liberal error allowance. However, to permit advancement with no concern for errors is not likely to build skill.

If accuracy is the goal, then the student should be required to repeat the paragraph until it can be done within the time allowed and within the error limit determined by the teacher. For example, if a student's goal is 45 words a minute and the error limit is 2%, then the student will be allowed to make one error only (45 × 0.02 = 0.90). If the timing is for two minutes, the allowance will be two errors (45 × 0.02 × 2 = 1.80).

Whichever goal is selected, students should be permitted to preview the paragraphs as well as to practise the material in which they have made errors.

Foreword to the Second Edition

The number of timings in this second edition has been increased from eighty to ninety-two. Forty-two of these are new and four others, which appeared in the first edition, have been considerably revised.

The forty-six timings which remain from the first edition have been updated and fully metricated.

In addition, the section on drills has been increased to three pages and contains new specialized drill material.

DRILLS

Set margins for a 60-stroke line and type each line at least three times.

Individual Finger Drills

```
1.     f r f r fr fr frf frf j u j u ju ju juj juj frf juj frf juj
2.     d e d e de de ded ded k i k i ki ki kik kik ded kik ded kik
3.     s w s w sw sw sws sws l o l o lo lo lol lol sws lol sws lol
4.     a q a q aq aq aqa aqa ; p ; p ;p ;p ;p; ;p; aqa ;p; aqa ;p;
5.     frfrf jujuj fgfgf jhjhj deded kikik swsws lolol aqaqa ;p;p;
6.     f t f t ft ft ftf ftf j y j y jy jy jyj jyj ftf jyj ftf jyj
7.     a;qpa; slwosl dkeidk fjrufj ghtygh fjrufj dkeidk slwosl a;q
8.     f v f v fv fv fvf fvf j m j m jm jm jmj jmj fvf jmj fvf jmj
9.     d c d c dc dc dcd dcd k , k , k, k, k,k k,k dcd k,k dcd k,k
10.    s x s x sx sx sxs sxs l . l . l. l. l.l l.l sxs l.l sxs l.l
11.    a z a z az az aza aza ; / ; / ;/ ;/ ;/; ;/; aza ;/; aza ;/;
12.    f b f b fb fb fbf fbf j n j n jn jn jnj jnj fbf jnj fbf jnj
13.    fvfvf jmjmj dcdcd k,k,k sxsxs l.l.l azaza ;/;/; fbfbf jnjnj
14.    a;z/a; slx.sl dkc,dk fjvmfj ghbngh fjvmfj dkc,dk slx.sl a;z
15.    frfvf jujmj ftfbf jyjnj dedcd kik,k swsxs lol.l aqaza ;p;/;
```

DRILLS

THE GREAT DEPRESSION — II

Even today there are a good number of people who still wonder what could have caused the great depression that hit Canada and other nations of the world in 1929. The late 1920s were considered good years but there were a few danger signs that most people failed to see. In the United States, factories were producing far more goods than they were able to sell with the result that goods were being stockpiled. In Canada, too, there was a danger sign in the huge crops of wheat that could not be sold because other countries had good crop years. The sale of wheat was critical for Canada because its survival was based on its ability to sell a large part of what it produced to other nations.

When the "crash" came in 1929, the export market collapsed as other nations put up trade barriers in an effort to protect their own industries. Most of Canada's primary industries cut back production or closed completely and this, in turn, affected almost every facet of the economy. As the supply of money declined, fewer goods were produced or sold because people could not afford to buy them.

Conditions around the world started to improve in 1935 but very slowly. Even by 1939, the year that war was declared, there were still more than half a million people without jobs. The miracle that returned the country to full prosperity, war, was not the choice that most people would wish for, but it was war that got the factories running two and even three shifts a day, seven days a week, to produce the goods and weapons needed to defeat the enemy. Since the war, many steps have been taken to insure that another depression does not occur because anyone who lived through it does not want to see history repeat itself.

Stroking Drills

16.   fff jjj ddd kkk sss lll aaa ;;; sss lll ddd kkk fff jjj ggg hhh
17.   frf juj ded kik sws lol aqa ;p; sws lol ded kik frf juj ftf jyj
18.   fvf jmj dcd k,k sxs l.l aza ;/; sxs l.l dcd k,k fvf jmj fbf jnj
19.   frf juj ftf jyj fgf jhj fbf jnj fvf jmj frftf jujyj fvfbf jmjnj
20.   abcdefghijklmnopqrstuvwxyz abcdefghijklmnopqrstuvwxyz abcdefghi

Vertical Row Drills

21.   fff jjj frf juj fvf jmj frfvf jujmj fvfrf jmjuj rrr uuu vvv mmm
22.   ddd kkk ded kik dcd k,k dedcd kik,k dcded k,kik eee iii ccc ,,,
23.   sss lll sws lol sxs l.l swsxs lol.l sxsws l.lol www ooo xxx ...
24.   aaa ;;; aqa ;p; aza ;/; aqaza ;p;/; azaqa ;/;p; qqq ppp zzz ///
25.   ftf jyj fgf jhj fbf jnj ftfgf jyjhj fbfgf jnjhj ttt yyy bbb nnn

Space Bar Drills

26.   a ; s l d k f j g h f j d k s l a ; s l d k f j g h f j d k s l
27.   aa ;; ss ll dd kk ff jj gg hh ff jj dd kk ss ll aa ;; ss ll dd
28.   aa bb cc dd ee ff gg hh ii jj kk ll mm nn oo pp qq rr ss tt uu
      vv ww xx yy zz
29.   a, b, c, d, e, f, g, h, i, j, k, l, m, n, o, p, q, r, s, t, u,
      v, w, x, y, z   (one space after the comma)
30.   a. b. c. d. e. f. g. h. i. j. k. l. m. n. o. p.
      q. r. s. t. u. v. w. x. y. z.   (two spaces after the
                                                          period)

DRILLS

THE GREAT DEPRESSION — I

One of the worst disasters that any nation had to face struck Canada in 1929. The depression that hit our country as well as those of many other nations was one of the worst the world has ever known. It is only in the past few years that stories of what happened to people who lived during the period known as "the Dirty Thirties" have been coming out. It would seem that most people who lived through it would prefer to forget that it ever happened.

Canada, like most other nations, was totally unprepared for what followed. Factories closed their doors when they could not sell all the goods they produced and this threw thousands of men and women out of work. Then the stores closed their doors or laid off their help because no one could afford to buy the goods they were selling. Young people just out of school were forced to walk the streets looking for any job they could find. The provinces and cities and towns could not collect enough money from taxes to support the number of their people that were on welfare. The federal government gave large grants of money to try and help but even this was not enough. Thousands of young men took to riding the rails in the hope of finding opportunity somewhere else. Most of them were unsuccessful and some spent years riding the rails from one end of the country to the other.

To add to the problem, the southern part of the western provinces was hit with the worst drought in their history. In some areas there was little or no rain for four years; in others, as long as eight years. The sun burned the earth to dust and the winds blew the rich topsoil away. Hundreds of families were forced to abandon their homes as their farms turned into deserts. Many simply walked away and never came back. At the peak of the depression in 1934, there were more than one million people without jobs.

DRILLS

Shift Key Drills

31. fF; dD; sS; aA; gG; rR; tT; eE; wW; qQ; vV; bB; cC; xX; zZ;

32. jJa kKa lLa ::a hHa uUa yYa iIa oOa pPa mMa nNa ,,a /?a

33. Fran Gigi Vic Bob Dora Eddy Cora Steve Wilma Xavier Alan Quent Zora Ruth Tom

34. Judy Kim Lorne Paul Olga Iona Ulla Yolande Mike Nancy Heather

35. Mr. W. L. Turner, B. A., M. A., received his Ph. D. yesterday.

One Hand Drills

36. asdfgfdsa ;lkjhjkl; asdfgfdsa ;lkjhjkl; asdfgfdsa ;lkjhjkl;

37. aqa sws ded frf ftf fgf fbf fvf dcd sxs aza qq zz ww xx ee cc

38. ;p; lol kik juj jyj jhj jnj jmj k,k l.l ;/; pp // oo .. ii ,,

39. we at as red cat vet axe adz test text vase dear fewer zebra

40. in on up no ill mop ilk nil yon milk kiln mini holly hippy

Number Drills

41. 1 and 2 and 3 and 4 and 5 and 6 and 7 and 8 and 9 and 10

42. 2 or 4 or 6 or 8 or 10 or 12 or 14 or 16 or 18 or 20 or 22

43. 1 and 3 and 5 and 7 and 9 and 11 and 13 and 15 and 17 and 19

44. 10 or 20 or 30 or 40 or 50 or 60 or 70 or 80 or 90 or 100

45. 15 times 4 equals 60 minus 10 equals 50 plus 4 equals 54 divided by 2 equals 27. Right?

FROM SEA TO SEA

Canada is today a nation which stretches from sea to sea but there was a time in the early 1850s when our western border might never have gone beyond the Red River Valley in what is now the province of Manitoba. Few people at that time believed that the plains were of any value. In fact, the report of one of the early surveys indicated that the plains were arid and useless. It was the fear that the United States would annex the land in order to provide a land route to their new territory in Alaska that led the government to buy it from the Hudson's Bay Company.

One of the most important factors that enabled our country to stretch from sea to sea was the building of a railway that joined the colony of British Columbia with the new nation of Canada. The railway was to be built in ten years but shortly after work had begun, a scandal erupted when it was learned that the leader of the governing Conservative party had accepted funds from one of the builders of the railway. In the election that followed, his party was defeated with the result that very little work was done during the next five years. When the party regained power, urged on by threats of withdrawal from union by the colony of British Columbia, a more active policy of building was made and seven years later, in 1885, the railway was finally completed. It was an outstanding job, even for that time, to find and build a route through the Rocky Mountains.

The railway, which is still the longest in North America, opened the west to settlement and in the two decades that followed, more than two million people moved in to settle the "useless" plains.

SPEED SENTENCES

5-STROKE WORDS

1. The bus will not be here for at least an hour yet. 10
2. Will you stop by and take me with you to the city?
3. I carried the pail of water over to the ball game.

4. I do not feel that it would be a good idea to go there. 11
5. If you see her before I do, will you tell her our plan?
6. The list that you gave them was sent over to our house.

7. Do you know if they will be able to play with our ball club? 12
8. She should send them a cheque at once and pay off this debt.
9. Can I leave these tickets with you until I return next week?

10. A few of the young men in our club will be at the fair this week. 13
11. He will have a job at the new city bank when it opens next month.
12. Do you still feel that you can carry all these boxes by yourself?

13. This is the time of the year when we check all the stock in our store. 14
14. Do you know if Sue found the watch she lost at the picnic last Sunday?
15. The sudden storm last night forced a good number of cars off the road.

SPEED SENTENCES

THE SQUIRREL

Of all the many types of wildlife that exist in Canada, one of the most common fur-bearing animals, the one most familiar to people, even the city dweller, is the squirrel. Although the ones that inhabit the towns and cities appear to be of two different kinds, they are, in fact, of the same family, as the black is merely a colour variation of the grey.

The red squirrel is a cheerful, chattering inhabitant of the less populated regions, somewhat smaller than the grey, with reddish fur on top, a black line down the sides, and a white belly. The red is familiar to summer cottagers as it darts about the undergrowth or perches on a bough to scold long and loudly over the slightest imposition.

The most interesting member of the squirrel family is the flying squirrel which has a silky, brown coat and a white belly. They are fairly common in the holiday areas, though seldom seen since they are active only at night, but once in a while someone may hear the soft but solid thump of one landing on a cottage roof or, if lucky, see this charming animal gliding downward in the twilight from one tree to another. It glides by means of a loose fold of skin which extends from the front feet to the hind legs, and a flattened tail which also helps in gliding.

Most people, at one time or another, have seen some of these creatures running about collecting and burying acorns in the fall. One squirrel is capable of gathering more than a thousand nuts, but there is some doubt that it really remembers where it has hidden this food. Luck more than cleverness leads the squirrel to these caches when they are covered with snow. Unlike some of the other fur-bearing animals, squirrels do not hibernate in winter though they do remain in their trees during storms or extreme cold.

Speed Sentences — Continued

5-STROKE WORDS

16. We will send you our order for the shirts and ties by the end of this week. 15

17. Take all the old cards from the file, count them, and put them on the desk.

18. They lost all they owned when their house caught fire while they were away.

19. A trust fund was set up to take care of the two boys both now and in the future. 16

20. The bank has given me some extra time to pay off the loan that I made last year.

21. Our files show that the account you asked about is more than one month past due.

22. Very few of the men want to move to a new city when the plant here is closed in June. 17

23. The price that they were asking for their house was much more than I was able to pay.

24. We will need two young college men to help us with our survey next spring and summer.

25. Just fill in the blanks on the front of this sheet and return it to us as soon as you can. 18

26. Did you give the store a cheque for the shoes and socks you bought from them last Tuesday?

27. We have not yet found a copy of the rare book that you asked for but we shall keep trying.

SPEED SENTENCES 2

THE BEAVER

If any animal is responsible for the growth of a country, it is the beaver, which has well and truly earned its position as a symbol of Canada. It was the fur of the beaver that lured the French and British into opening the wilderness, and upon it was built the great era of the voyageurs.

The beaver is the largest rodent in North America, with adults having a mass of 31 kg or more. They have four strong, orange-coloured teeth, two in the upper jaw and two in the lower, which are for gnawing. The forefeet are armed with claws used for digging, combing their fur, and for handling the sticks, stones, and mud used in their endless construction work. The hind feet are webbed between the five toes and, with the flat, trowel-shaped tail, provide locomotion in swimming.

The beaver lives in lodges, in family groups called colonies, on the shores of lakes or near dams built on streams, though beavers living on lakes may build no dams at all. Entrances to the lodges are located below the surface of the water, with a passage leading upward to dry, warm living quarters safely tucked away above the water level in the heart of interlaced branches, twigs, stones, and mud.

Beavers are entirely vegetarian and are noted for their tree-cutting ability, gnawing at the base of a tree with their incisors until it falls of its own force or is pushed over by the wind. In this regard, a beaver is not as wise as is commonly supposed for frequently a tree will fall in the opposite direction to where the beaver wants it. Once a tree is downed, the beaver chews off succulent branches and stores them near the lodge entrance where they may be used as food when ice covers the surface and they cannot emerge to forage.

Speed Sentences — Continued

5-STROKE WORDS

28. I would like to buy a new suit when I am in town as the brown one that I now have is quite old. — 19

29. If you would keep your boat until the end of the week, I would then be able to buy it from you.

30. Even though we had a loss last year, our first year, we expect to make a nice profit this year.

31. We will need a girl who can type at a high rate of speed and with good control to fill this new job. — 20

32. It took two men more than two hours to clean up the debris that was left on the road near our place.

33. Once our stock has been tagged we will hold a big sale before the new fall lines come on the market.

34. Would you send me a copy of the floor plan so that I might look at it once more before I make up my mind? — 21

35. It will take a party of men more than a week to clean up the damage caused by the fire we had last night.

36. I am happy to hear that you and your wife have agreed to buy the old stone house I showed you last night.

37. As I expect to be here for a few days, I would like to know how much it will cost me to rent one of your cars. — 22

38. If they will let us buy this new machine, we will be able to cut the time down by at least four or five hours.

39. We think that you should put in a claim for the seven cases of soap that were lost when the truck turned over.

KING OF THE FOREST

Canada is a heavily forested country with thousands of lakes and rivers. With the largest proportion of its population living within a narrow band that follows the southern boundary of the country, millions of hectares of forest have remained relatively untouched. As a result, the woods abound with wildlife which makes it a paradise for the hunter. Of the many varieties of animals found there, one of the most sought after of the large game animals is the moose.

The moose, which could easily qualify in the minds of some people as the king of the forest, is one of the most exciting animals to view. It is not uncommon for one to step across a northern highway or stand in full view while foraging for lily roots in a pond or the shallows of a lake. Unlike the deer, the moose prefers to live in well-watered forests and is found throughout the northern wilderness of the Canadian Shield though, on occasion, it may be seen in heavily forested areas further south.

The big creature can, when it wants to, move with surprisingly little noise in the thickest bush, but more often than not will crash through saplings with all the noise and strength of an army tank, for a big bull may stand about two metres at the withers. Its head is long and narrow, with a flexible muzzle, and is crowned with a wide pair of flattened antlers known as a rack. The rack is shed each year and grown anew every summer, as are those of the deer.

To have seen a moose shouldering out of a lake, water streaming from its dark brown flanks, then standing proudly with antlered head held high before turning to vanish majestically into the forest, is a sight one will long remember.

ACCURACY SENTENCES

5-STROKE WORDS

1. A study should be made before any action is taken. — 10
2. He selected a number of topics for our discussion.
3. I resigned because it was an impossible situation.

4. We plan to take our holidays in December and go skiing. — 11
5. In my opinion, the parcel should be shipped by express.
6. Just complete and return the enclosed application form.

7. He was quite late in making his mortgage payment this month. — 12
8. What is the foreign exchange rate today on American dollars?
9. She sincerely regrets any inconvenience this has caused you.

10. Do you have any reason for suspecting him of stealing the papers? — 13
11. The funds were distributed to various welfare groups in the city.
12. Extreme caution must be taken by workers when handling chemicals.

13. We would recommend that you travel by train rather than by automobile. — 14
14. We cannot quote you specific figures until we receive further details.
15. I received a personal invitation yesterday to attend their conference.

THE EASTERN ARCTIC PATROL

Compared with the old days of fragile sailing ships, sea travel in the Arctic is now almost routine, even though a journey through ice-choked waters is still far from uneventful. It is a task that requires skill and patience for even the massive, steel ships of today can suffer great damage from the ice. Today there are a large number of ships that make regular calls to busy harbours, as well as smaller vessels that travel to the small posts along the seemingly endless coastline, but the small ports and outposts depend largely upon the Eastern Arctic Patrol for their supplies.

This Patrol, which has been made each year for almost fifty years, has a long and honourable history. At one time, it not only brought in all the supplies needed for a whole year, but it also carried a doctor and a few scientists who spent their time studying the frozen wastes of the north. The arrival of the ship was always a big occasion for the white residents and for the Inuit who would come from some distance.

In the past, the doctor tried to provide as much medical help as he could for there were no services this far north, but today there is a full medical team which, besides looking after the general health of the people, carries out a complete chest survey in order to try and control tuberculosis which is quite prevalent in the Arctic. Today, as well, there are even social workers on hand, so that if someone has to leave his home for treatment on the outside, they arrange to have the other members of the family cared for.

Some of the functions of the Patrol have now been taken over by other agencies, and some of the places it once called upon on its journey of over nineteen thousand kilometres are serviced by planes, but the Patrol still performs an important service to the lonely islands of the high Arctic.

Accuracy Sentences — Continued

5-STROKE WORDS

16. I shall let you know, as soon as possible, the outcome of the negotiations.

15

17. I am very concerned with the excessive expenses we have been having lately.

18. Someone removed the accident file from this drawer without letting me know.

19. He has just accepted a new position in sales promotion with a major oil company.

16

20. A large number of people attended the concert held in the auditorium last night.

21. The expansion plans for your organization will have to be postponed temporarily.

22. I have a business proposal to discuss with you if you are free on Thursday afternoon.

17

23. There were a large number of pieces missing in the shipment we received this morning.

24. Do you believe that further changes will be necessary before we can begin production?

25. Extreme care is essential in order to insure that the crystals are not damaged in transit.

18

26. Their company made an assignment early last month and now operates under a public trustee.

27. We must have detailed specifications before we can proceed any further with this contract.

ACCURACY SENTENCES 2

BUSH FLYING

The growth and development of the Northwest Territories have moved at a much slower pace than that of the Yukon because of the lack of transportation routes to the outside world. Unlike the Yukon, which has had a railway line since the turn of the century, the first line in the Territories was completed just a few years ago. The only trunk highway that is open both summer and winter was built less than twenty years ago. Prior to that, passengers and supplies were brought in over winter roads that were built on ice over water and muskeg or by airplane.

This is the land that gave birth to bush flying, about which so many tales have been written. This is good flying country for there are no high mountains as in the Yukon, and the thousands of lakes of the Canadian Shield provide many landing places in both winter and summer. Although aircraft have often been forced down because of bad weather or because they lost their way and ran out of fuel, the large number of safe landing areas, especially above the tree line, virtually assures that no aircraft is seriously damaged or its passengers hurt. From this point of view, the Arctic is quite safe for flying in light planes provided that in winter one is well dressed for a night on the barrens.

Because of the limited number of good roads, many towns still depend upon the airplane to a large extent. Most of the larger communities have airports with permanent runways which can be used all year round. In the smaller villages and Arctic outposts, the planes land either on the sea or on nearby lakes or, in winter, on ice strips marked out for ski planes. Still, there may be as much as two months in the year, during break-up in the spring and freeze-up in the fall, when a community without a permanent airstrip is cut off from the outside world.

Accuracy Sentences — Continued

5-STROKE WORDS

28. You are entitled to a trade discount in addition to the usual cash discount for prompt payment. — 19

29. This letter will acknowledge receipt of your cheque in full payment of the balance outstanding.

30. Are you still interested in purchasing a modern, attractive house overlooking the river valley?

31. Please fill in and return the enclosed proxy form in the stamped envelope provided for this purpose. — 20

32. According to the report we received, your transport was badly damaged in the collision last evening.

33. Our recommendation is that you postpone any further investment until the market becomes more stable.

34. Although I have not had an opportunity to see the play, I understand that it was exceptionally well done. — 21

35. If you are agreeable, we would like you to represent us in current contract negotiations with management.

36. Beginning next month, our advertisements will appear regularly in four of the largest national magazines.

37. The insurance adjusters will be sending us a complete, detailed report of the damage done to our uptown store. — 22

38. Your last order was shipped yesterday morning by truck transport and you should receive it before the weekend.

39. He was quite an intelligent young man but, unfortunately, he lacked the experience required for this position.

THE SNOW HOUSE

The igloo, or more accurately, the snow house, for "igloo" means any kind of house, is an invention peculiar to Canada and it is widely used in the eastern and central parts of the Arctic.

A typical, dome-shaped snow house can be erected by an experienced person in about an hour. It is made from hard, wind-packed snow cut into blocks about 0.9 m long. The blocks are not placed in layers but in a spiral that gradually slopes inward, with one last hole at the top filled by a key block. Most snow houses are built from the inside. The packed snow is cut away from the floor with slightly more than one-half of the area left raised. This raised portion serves as a sleeping platform and is covered with layers of caribou skin for warmth.

Unless the snow house is constructed as a temporary shelter, it will have a second, usually smaller igloo, which serves as a porch. The low entrance, which requires one to enter on hands and knees, was designed that way to discourage any large, curious animals from entering. A hole is usually left in the roof to allow the smoke of the lamp and the fire to escape. Blubber burned in a saucer-shaped lamp carved from soapstone provides the light. Caribou skins are used as doors and windows, if any, and are made from clear ice or the gut of an animal. If there are two or more houses grouped together, they would be joined by a snow passage to enable the inhabitants to visit each other without having to go outside.

Although the snow house is romantic and picturesque in nature, it is not warm enough today for people who wear factory-made clothing. Within a few years, with the continuing advances being made in housing technology, the snow house, except as a temporary home, will become virtually obsolete.

SKILL-BUILDING PARAGRAPHS

5-STROKE WORDS

1. In order to raise funds to finance our latest civic project, we will be holding a street dance on Friday night. Will you help us with the organization? 30

2. Almost every person in town attended the track meet held here last week. It was only through the efforts of people like yourself that this meet was a success. 32

3. Ever since our full-page ad began to appear each week in the local paper, our sales have increased many times over. Thank you again for helping us prepare this program. 34

4. We have just received a large stock of British woollens and would suggest, while our display is still complete, that you visit us and see our exciting new fabrics for fall and winter. 36

5. If you are not fully satisfied with the clothing you may return any of the articles, provided this is done within a reasonable time, and provided that the goods have not been soiled or used. 38

THE INUIT — II

The main unit in Inuit has always been the family. Several families might group together for hunting and marriage but, otherwise, the group structure has been informal. Until the settlers came, the Inuit was a nomad who moved both in summer and winter to where the hunting and fishing was best.

Their main diet was the animals of the sea — the seal, the walrus, and the whale — and very little was ever wasted. As well as provide adequate food for all, these animals supplied the oil used in stone lamps for both heat and light. The skin of the seal was used for summer clothing as well as for covering boats and tents. The skin of the bearded seal was cut into long strips for traces on the dog sled. Ivory from the walrus and the narwhal, as well as whale bones, was made into weapons, instruments, and runners for sleds.

Almost as important as the sea animals was the caribou which has sometimes been called a walking department store. Not only was the meat a favourite food, but the caribou skin made the best winter clothing and the best rugs for the sleeping platforms of the snow house. Inuit clothing is so well designed for the climate that modern scientists, after years of research, have not been able to improve upon it or even equal it with manufactured cloth.

Life, however, is changing for the Inuit as industry moves further and further north for he has shown that he is able to handle the complex equipment that the newcomers have brought in. The Inuit is already world-famous for prints and soapstone carvings and may well play an even bigger role in the life of Canada in the years to come.

| 1 | 2 | 3 | 4 | 5 | 6 | 7 | 8 | 9 | 10 | 11 | 12 | 13 | 14 |

TIMED WRITINGS 83 — NORTHERN TERRITORIES

Skill-Building Paragraphs — Continued

5-STROKE WORDS

6. Please complete and return the enclosed form at your earliest convenience. This data is needed to bring our present records up to date in order that our store may serve you better in the years ahead. 40

7. You may be assured that all our merchandise meets the highest standards of quality. If, after you have had an opportunity to examine our goods carefully, you do not agree, we will be glad to grant you a refund. 42

8. A memo just received from our head office states that the sales manager will arrive here on Thursday morning to outline the changes that have been proposed for our zone. All sales staff are expected to be at the meeting. 44

9. Over the past four years, our lost and found department has accumulated a large collection of unclaimed items. We plan to hold an auction to dispose of as many items as we can. The proceeds will be turned over to some charity. 46

10. I would like to draw your attention to the new campaign for funds that is now on in our city. If the service agencies are to continue their fine work among those needing assistance, they will need your full support. Please give generously. 48

SKILL-BUILDING PARAGRAPHS 2

THE INUIT — I

More than five thousand years have passed since the last boatload of original settlers landed in our North with their few meagre belongings. They were the last of untold numbers who had for ages moved from Asia in search of a better place to live. Those who had come earlier had worked their way down the coast and out across the land, but this last group, the Inuit, moved over the top of the map and made the Arctic their home.

Some parts of their history have been pieced together from a few scattered remains that have been preserved by the Arctic cold, but even now there is still much to learn. No one knows exactly how many Inuit there were in Canada before the explorers arrived, probably twice as many as there are now, but many died from hunger as supplies of game dwindled or from disease brought in by the explorers. Then, as now, there were more Inuit in Alaska than there were in Canada.

Although there are a number of groups of Inuit spread across the north, there are no well-defined tribes. They can understand each other's speech, but there are marked differences in dialect as well as in dress, implements, and way of life. As they tend to move around with greater ease today, and to live and work with other Inuit, the differences are becoming less noticeable.

From the very first, these residents of the high Arctic have fascinated white people because they have managed to adapt to, and survive in, one of the most rugged climates in the world. Even though they have been studied and written about more often than any other group of similar size, there are still very few people who understand the workings of the Inuit mind.

Skill-Building Paragraphs — Continued

5-STROKE WORDS

11.   Thank you for your letter inquiring about the cost of our line of machines. We are pleased to say that we have been able to maintain our prices, despite rapidly rising costs, because of the way in which our machines have been accepted by industry.   50

12.   This coming summer, for the very first time, the school will be offering courses in basic shorthand and basic and advanced typewriting.

The courses will run for one hour each day for six weeks, starting the first Monday in July, and the cost will be quite low.   52

13.   The attached brief outlines a number of investment programs that we think may be of special interest to you. If you find one that meets your particular needs, please call us and one of our experts will gladly help you to work out your own personal investment program.   54

[Handwritten note next to 13: "Sept. 22 goal not achieved"]

SKILL-BUILDING PARAGRAPHS 3

THE BARRENS

The physical features of the Territories are almost as varied as Canada itself. The eastern two-thirds of the mainland lie in the Canadian Shield, a region of ancient mountains which had been worn down to its roots by time and the elements even before the last ice age arrived.

From the air, this part of the north looks like an endless expanse of flat land dotted with thousands of lakes. The terrain, however, is rough and hilly: hard rock with little soil and haphazard piles of rock and stone left by the retreating glaciers. There are moraines, countless hills of rock and clay which still mark the edges of glaciers that have long since disappeared, and eskers, long narrow ridges of sand and gravel that were dropped by streams which once poured through the melting ice caps. Though the lakes are many in this area, the rivers are few.

In the harsh loneliness of the barrens, people have found great beauty. They have been caught by the sense of space untouched by any trace of human achievement. In winter, it is an endless, even, white field of ice and thin, hard snow which takes on the warm colours of the changing sun. In summer, the rocks are warmly coloured and decorated with wild flowers which, in their very short life, burst forth in a violence of colour.

West of the Shield, to the mountains of the Yukon, the land is an extension of the flat lands of the prairies. It is mostly bush with thick soil and large lakes and rivers. In the future, this land may become quite valuable as the area is one of the best sedimentary oil-bearing regions of the continent. North of the mainland is a huge triangle of islands known as the Arctic Archipelago, most of which are unsettled and which still contain remnants of the great ice sheets which once covered almost all of Canada.

Skill-Building Paragraphs — Continued

5-STROKE WORDS

14. If you anticipate working part-time during the school year or full-time next summer, you may be required to prepare an income tax return.

    Our booklet is designed to show you in easy steps how to prepare your return. Free copies may be obtained from your school or guidance office. 56

15. Your order for two of our duplicating machines was received late yesterday. We expect a new shipment to arrive shortly and if it comes this week, we shall call you to arrange for delivery.

    The supplies that you bought for these machines are ready and will be delivered at the same time. 58

    [handwritten: Jan. 5 goal achieved]

16. Both of the manuals you inquired about in your recent letter have been out of print for several years and, unfortunately, we have no extra copies available at the present time.

    We would suggest that you contact some of the second-hand book dealers in your area as they might have copies in their stock. 60

    [handwritten: Jan. 7 goal achieved]

SKILL-BUILDING PARAGRAPHS 4

THE COLD DESERT

The Northwest Territories is by far the largest region in Canada, stretching thirty-two hundred kilometres across the map. On the west is the Yukon and on the south the three prairie provinces. The rest is bounded only by seas. The Territories include not only the vast mainland but the islands which reach north from it towards the Pole.

Despite its size, no part of our continent is so little known, and no part has produced more popular misconceptions about climate and living conditions. Those who think of the area as being snow-covered could not be more wrong for there is so little precipitation that most of the Arctic is classified as desert.

Approximately half of the mainland and all of the islands lie in what is called the Arctic; the remainder is sub-Arctic. The dividing line between the two is not the Arctic Circle, which is merely a line on the map that means little except that for one day each year the sun does not set on that line and for one day it does not rise. The only way to show the true division is by using the tree line, for the Arctic is a place where no trees will grow. The presence of trees depends upon the average summer temperature being at least 10°C or higher.

The Arctic region is the coldest part of our country even though it does not have the extremes in temperature that the Yukon has. What makes it so cold is the length of the severe winter. The temperature drops to minus thirty-five degrees Celsius in the middle of the three-month long twilight period in which the sun does not rise to warm the ground, and it remains there for a month or more. Over the past fifty years, however, the winters have been growing warmer as the glaciers continue to retreat northwards. It has been estimated that the permafrost and tree lines are moving north at the rate of approximately 96 km every hundred years.

Skill-Building Paragraphs — Continued

5-STROKE WORDS

17.   Please ship me two gross each of ballpoint pens in red and black and one gross in assorted colours. With school starting in less than a week, I would appreciate receiving them at your earliest convenience.

Jan. 5 goal not achieved

If you would forward them by parcel post I will pay the extra cost involved in sending them this way.   62

18.   We will be sending you a large supply of coloured posters and other display matter, within the next week or two, which we think will help you to make your store window quite attractive.

Jan. 7 goal achieved

A good portion of this material is free from advertisements of any particular brand of goods and should be of special value to you.   64

19.   Could you give us a quotation on ten dozen wool blankets, satin bound, in pastel shades? We will be opening a new fabric store this coming fall and we would like to offer these blankets as special inducements.

If you would like to discuss this matter in greater detail, we would be happy to speak to one of your representatives.   66

SKILL-BUILDING PARAGRAPHS 5   14

STERNWHEELERS IN THE YUKON

In days past, the rivers were the highways of the Yukon. They were almost the only way to travel, not only because of the dense bush, but because they were the easiest paths through the mountains. They were always frozen in winter, closed to passage except on foot or by dog sled. How long the water is open varies from year to year, but usually the main rivers are open to travel from May until October.

People sailed the rivers in frail canoes, in heavy open boats, on rafts, and in luxurious stern-wheel steamers. The big boats had to be specially constructed because of the shallows in the rivers, yet many were the times that boats big and small were stuck on the sandbars while the passengers anxiously watched as the crew tried to free them.

The sternwheelers started their career during the days of the Klondike gold rush. Dozens of these giant vessels were built to carry cargo from Dawson and Whitehorse to the mouth of the Yukon River. These steamboats all burned wood at a tremendous rate. One of the most important industries for people in the area was cutting wood and taking it to the river-bank where it would be bought by the captains as they made their way up and down the river.

The sternwheelers carried not only cargo, but passengers in considerable style. It took two days to go downstream and four days upstream against the current. In the early days, these boats were famous for their public rooms where miners gambled for large stakes paid in gold dust. They say it is still possible to pick up gold dust between the floor boards where the gamblers spilled it.

Now these craft ply the river no more. Modern bridges along the route bar their passage, and travellers now journey by car or airplane, but it is still possible to see a few of these steamboats along the shore of the Yukon River.

Skill-Building Paragraphs — Continued

5-STROKE WORDS

20. The company in charge of building our large apartment complex has just notified us that the land on which we propose to build will require special preparation before we can proceed.

Would you please send some of your engineers over to verify their findings and to find out exactly how much more it will cost us to carry on with our scheme. 68

21. The designs that you mailed to us will take approximately three months to make. We regret any hardship this delay may cause you but the fabric you want must be imported. We shall try to have the material rushed but we cannot promise anything definite.

If you would allow us to use another kind of fabric, we could have the drapes ready much sooner. 70

22. This letter will acknowledge receipt of the samples of new white bond paper asked for by our purchasing agent. Mr. Bronson is attending a conference out of town at the moment and we do not expect him back for several days, but we will bring this matter to his attention as soon as he returns.

Please accept our thanks for replying so promptly to this inquiry. 72

SKILL-BUILDING PARAGRAPHS 6   15

DAWSON CITY TODAY

Unlike most towns that die after a mining boom is over, Dawson City continued as the centre of government for the Yukon. For many long years the legend of the Klondike was kept alive in Dawson while the rest of the world forgot, but publicity has once again made the city famous and thousands come each year to see where the famous gold rush took place.

There is still a faded grandeur about the city. The grim trails that led to it still remain, much as they were when the first miners began their search for gold. Although many of the relics of the gold-rush days have been lost over the years, much of what remains has not been spoiled by civilization. Some of the old paddle wheelers that once brought men in by the hundreds have been preserved. The most famous theatre in the northwest, Dawson's Palace Grand, has been completely restored and in the summer its balconies echo again to the sounds of music and laughter.

Old stores which have not been used for many years have opened their doors again and are selling the wares that were bought in 1898. The banks, too, are open for business and their employees wear the costumes of the period. They still operate the "gold room" where fine gold from the creeks was tested, then melted into bars and shipped to the outside world.

Every year, on the 17th of August, the citizens of the Yukon celebrate Discovery Day and festivities are held in Dawson. The old fire engine, stolen from the city of Victoria by miners heading north to the gold fields, is shined up and everyone who can wears old-time dress. Of the many tourists who travel thousands of kilometres to visit Dawson, most come because they know that this is the birthplace of some of our most important history.

Skill-Building Paragraphs — Continued

5-STROKE WORDS

23. Several years ago I bought mining stock through your company. For the first year I received bulletins from you each month telling me how they were progressing but I have heard nothing for almost a year now.

    I have noticed, too, that they are not shown with the other stocks listed in the newspaper. Any assistance you can give me in this matter would be most welcome. 74

24. I have received a fair number of letters over the past few months from dealers in different sections of our area complaining about the length of time it takes our merchandise to reach them.

    Personally, I can see no reason why our deliveries should take more than a week. Would you look into this problem and let me know what, if anything, we can do to remedy this situation. 76

DAWSON CITY

The most popular route to the gold fields of the Klondike was an overland route from Skagway on the Pacific coast through several rugged mountain passes to the headwaters of the Yukon River. Once there, the men who came in the autumn and winter built their own boats or rafts in order to reach the boom town of Dawson. It was down river all the way, but the river was shallow and dangerous in places with many rapids and whirlpools. After weeks of struggle in the mountains, many of the voyagers suffered sudden disaster.

The wooden village of Dawson on the mud flats of the junction of two rivers soon became a roaring city. In addition to the miners, there were many others, among them the merchants, bankers and hotel-keepers, who thought that their fortunes could be made from the miners rather than from the mines.

Unlike many mining camps, there were women and even children, and they brought with them many luxuries of large cities: fine clothes and furniture, pianos and paintings. This was no longer a gold-mining camp. Dawson was a city of wealth and luxury, a city where fortunes were made on the creeks or in the gambling rooms. It was a city where poor men became rich overnight and where rich men lost their fortunes just as quickly.

Dawson was not a lawless town as one might expect, because the men of the North West Mounted Police were there to maintain order. Even though this was perhaps the wildest gold rush the world has ever seen, it was also the most law-abiding. Millions of dollars in gold were shipped out, and no attempt was ever made to steal any; no trading post was ever robbed; and no one ever bothered to lock his cabin door. On Sundays, the city was quiet except for the pealing of bells and the singing of hymns in churches.

NEWFOUNDLAND

Newfoundland is the oldest yet the newest part of our great country. The Vikings came briefly to its shores almost a thousand years ago; then its history lay silent for nearly five hundred years before Cabot landed, some five years after Columbus made his famous voyage to the new world.

The province itself is divided into two distinct physical parts. To the south is the island shaped like an arrowhead pointing westward into the mouth of the St. Lawrence River, its broad base washed by the ocean on the east. To the north, on the mainland, is Labrador which sits between the province of Quebec and the ocean. The two parts together give it an area that places it seventh in size among the ten provinces of our country.

Almost the whole of Newfoundland is located on a line north of the mainland cities of Quebec and Sudbury and, as a result, the weather is fairly cool all the year round. The winters on the other hand are not so severe as they are on the mainland because of the warming effect of the Gulf Stream as it moves northwards along the coast, and seldom does the temperature fall below zero.

The face of this province is a weather-beaten, craggy face eroded and deeply sculptured by the heavy ice masses advancing and retreating over many thousands of years. The wind, rain and sea have also combined over the ages to nibble its coastline into an island-dotted wall deeply indented with hundreds of bays and fjords of all sizes.

The towns, cities and villages on the island cling, for the most part, to the sea and shun the dark and lonely interior where dense forests of spruce and pine stand amid the lonely lakes and brooks, the bald rocks and muskeg that cover so much of the land.

THE SEARCH FOR GOLD

The gold in the Klondike creeks and rivers had been crumbling from a million different rocks since long before people came on the earth. It had been washed down from the hillsides over countless centuries, and now it lay in the form of pure nuggets mixed with gravel waiting to be sifted out by men with dreams of riches.

The sifting was not a complicated process. The simplest way, though not the most profitable, was to scoop up some of the yellow gravel and water in a pan and to swirl it carefully to spill out the lighter sand and gravel while the heavy gold nuggets remained at the bottom. Many men dug shafts into the frozen hillside, slowly thawed the ground, and carted out the rich muck to sift for gold. They built wooden sluice boxes and ran water through them to sift for the precious metal. Sometimes the water was carried great distances in wooden troughs or, later, by metal pipe.

No one knows how much gold was taken from the Klondike, but it was worth more than a quarter of a billion dollars. Most of it was uncovered after the initial rush was over by large machines on dredges which were capable of finding gold easily missed by prospectors using crude methods and home-made equipment.

The Klondike rush had one thing in common with most other mineral rushes. No matter how rich a strike they made, the miners were always looking for an even richer find. When much of the easy gold had been found, the boom was over and most of the people attracted by the thought of quick fortunes departed. Gold is still being taken today in the Yukon, though mostly by heavy machinery, but it is still possible with patience and a little expert guidance to find that magic flash in a pan of Klondike gravel.

THE FIRST COLONY

On the 5th day of August, in the year 1583, Newfoundland formally became the first colonial possession of England. On that day, Sir Humphrey Gilbert read to the assembled people of the harbour of St. John's his Royal Commission which granted for the Queen and for himself and his heirs, the harbour and the land around for 200 leagues in all directions. The first simple laws of the colony were also enacted that day. The first decreed that worship should be according to the Church of England; the second, that any action against the Queen would be considered high treason; the third, that any person who spoke ill of the Queen would lose his ship, his goods and his ears.

Sir Humphrey's claim to Newfoundland was ironic in that it was not his intention to settle there. Originally he had planned only to stop for provisions before heading for warmer lands in the south but, because of the lateness of the season, he did not feel he could go any further. This was the second blow that doomed his whole mission to failure. The first happened only two days after leaving England when the largest ship in his fleet of five deserted to try its hand at piracy. The third blow occurred during his short stay on the island. A large number of the members of his mission became ill and had to be sent home on another ship. The fourth blow, a real tragedy, happened shortly after they left the island when the second largest ship of the fleet suddenly went down off Sable Island with the loss of all hands.

Thoroughly discouraged, and faced with a sullen crew, Sir Humphrey set off for home with his two remaining ships. However, just off the horizon of the coast of England, a severe storm struck and the ship carrying Sir Humphrey went down and all hands were lost.

THE LURE OF YUKON GOLD

In the years that followed the discovery of gold in the Cariboo, men continued to pan the gravel shores of rivers and creeks in the Yukon in search of this elusive mineral. Many became discouraged and quit, but just enough gold was found each year to keep the more determined searching for the legendary mother lode.

Suddenly on one drowsy summer afternoon in 1897, as three prospectors were resting by a creek called the Bonanza, one of the men noticed the metallic glint of gold as he lay down to drink some water. They scooped the gravel into their pans and patiently swished away the dirt and sand. At the bottom of one pan alone, they uncovered gold worth more than fourteen dollars. It was an exciting moment, but it was nothing compared to the wealth which they and others were soon to discover in that small corner of the Yukon known as the Klondike.

At first, many of the veteran prospectors could not believe their story but, within days of registering their claim, the rush was on. The lure of gold was like a magnet, and it attracted people from all corners of the world. The centre of the rush was a little village called Dawson which did not even exist the day of the great discovery, but within a year it became the largest Canadian city in the west.

Although men by the thousands left their jobs and their homes to search for gold, most had no idea of the tremendous difficulties that faced them. There were no roads or railways, and the only open route was a safe but tedious journey of more than 2720 km along the Yukon River. Because this method was too slow for many, some tried to cross the glacier which separates the Yukon from the ocean; others tried to scale the mountains; still others tried to fight their way north through dense forest and swamp. Nearly all of these failed to reach the gold fields.

THE FISHING ADMIRAL

In the years that followed Cabot's landing in Newfoundland, no serious attempts were made to bring settlers to the island. No one knows exactly when the first permanent settlements were made, but it is generally believed that they were started by the English fishermen.

The fishermen from the other countries had little need for land, except as a place to store their supplies, for they usually salted the fish that they caught. English fishermen, on the other hand, cured their catch by drying it to a hard consistency under the sun. To cure their fish properly, then, the English needed land. This need for land resulted in much competition between crews for the best sites and led, as may be expected, to disputes over ownership of land. Out of this mad scramble for land came the first real, though crude, attempt at establishing a system of law and order.

The first captain to arrive at a cove was made the lord of the harbour or, as he was later called, the Admiral or Fishing Admiral. This position normally lasted the whole fishing season, but more often than not might was right. The Admiral had to decide matters in which he himself might be involved and which he would, naturally, decide in his own favour. Anyone who earned the displeasure of the lord could have his place on the beach taken from him or he could be fined and even whipped.

Though fair in principle, this system of law and order was unjust to the extent that the skipper, no matter how ignorant or debased he might be, had the power of life or death over hundreds of people. Almost 150 years were to pass before a just legal system was set up to look after the interests of the settlers who had come to this new land.

THE NORTHLAND

Approximately one-third of the total area of Canada is found north of the ten provinces and stretches northward to the Pole. This cold, and to some people desolate, land is still today one of the last frontiers of the world. The smaller of the two territories that make up our northland, the Yukon, which borders the state of Alaska, is mostly sub-arctic, and its weather is not nearly as harsh as many people suppose. While it is true that no place in the world has two such extremes of temperature between summer and winter, the Yukon is very dry, and even the snowfall is quite moderate.

As in all northern parts of our country, the winter days are short, but the summer, though short in duration, has long hours of sunshine which are not only quite pleasant but important to the farmers and the market gardeners. The biggest problems for growing crops are the light rainfall, only about 15 cm in summer, and the short growing season, often less than two months in length.

Although the story of the Yukon goes back at least six thousand years, it has only been in recent years that experts have been able to fit together some of the missing pieces of its history. We now know that no less than nine waves of nomadic hunters and fishers have come from Asia over the ages, but it will take much more patient work before we know what happened in the thousands of years before the land was first opened by white explorers and fur traders.

Until the closing years of the 19th century, it appeared that the Yukon was unlikely to find an important place in the history books of our country, but the discovery of gold at Bonanza Creek started the greatest gold rush the world has ever seen and changed forever the character of this land.

THE BEOTHUCKS I

There is no blacker page in the history of the province of Newfoundland than the extermination of the aborigines, a race known as the Beothucks. All that remains of the tribe today may be found in the provincial museum — the skeleton of a full-grown male approximately 180 cm tall, the mummified bodies of two children, and some simple artifacts.

The Beothucks were an ancient people with an old stone-age culture who are now believed to have arrived some eight or nine thousand years ago shortly after the end of the last great ice age that covered most of our continent. They had a language of their own, not one syllable of which had any resemblance to that of any of the known mainland races.

The excessive use by this tribe of a paint made from red ochre gave them the name of Red Indians, a name that was later extended to all of the Indians of our continent. They used the ochre to paint themselves for the hunt, to paint their tools, their weapons, and even the bodies of their dead.

The Beothucks were a people of average height, though there are recorded instances of giants 210 cm in height, who dressed in animal skins often adorned with trinkets or carved bone, stone, or sea shells. They lived primarily by hunting and fishing, their weapons consisting of bows and arrows, stone axes, knives, and wooden clubs. During the summer, they lived by the sea in wigwams of skin or bark where they hunted seals, caught salmon and other fish, and collected the eggs of sea birds. With the coming of the colder weather, they moved their homes inland to the shelter of the forests where they remained for the whole winter.

THE ALASKA HIGHWAY

With the end of the gold rush, peace settled once again over the Yukon. Big dredges still worked the river beds, and prospectors ranged the hills and valleys, but no minerals in the quantity needed to start a new boom were found. Then in 1942, because of the war, it was decided that a safe inland route to Alaska would be needed to combat the threat of enemy submarines at sea.

With the permission of Canada, the United States built a highway that stretched twenty-four hundred kilometres across the rugged interior of British Columbia from the end of the railway line into the heart of Alaska. To the oldtimers it seemed like the gold rush again, but this time the atmosphere was different. Life was not the easy, carefree life of Dawson at its peak, but the grim reality of war as men and huge machines churned through the muskeg and bush.

No road like it had been built before. Most of the ground was permanently frozen below the surface. There was bad muskeg everywhere — frozen, marshy land on which men said no road could be built. Sometimes, the road had to detour along ridges and, at other times, great trenches had to be dug and filled with rock and gravel. In places, brush 1.5 m in depth was piled on the ground and gravel put on top so that the permafrost would not melt and heave the roadbed.

Despite the bitter winter weather and the vicious mosquitoes of summer, rivers and streams were bridged and rockfalls cleared. One of the biggest problems the men had to face was water seepage from the hills which froze as it crossed the road and formed impassable barriers of ice. What some had said could not be done, or that would take years to build, was completed in a little over seven months by an army of fifteen thousand workers.

THE BEOTHUCKS II

The Beothucks were the people that Cabot met when he first landed on the island of Newfoundland, but their numbers declined swiftly in the years that followed as they were hunted and shot on sight both by white men and by Indians of other tribes. The early settlers had had a measure of success in making friends with them, but their habit of pilfering axes and other gear finally caused the settlers to take more drastic action against them, action which led, in the end, to their extinction.

Attempts were made by the settlers in later years to establish more humane relations with the small numbers that still remained, but the efforts came too late. The final chapter was written in 1823 when two men out hunting came upon a small Indian camp. A hostile move by one of the Indians forced the hunters to shoot and kill him; a second drowned while trying to escape across the thin ice of a nearby river. Inside the wigwam, the hunters found a Beothuck mother and two of her daughters in a state of near starvation.

All three women were taken back, fed, and cared for. When they had recovered, they were given food and gifts to take back to the other members of their tribe. The three women returned several weeks later and indicated that they were not able to find any trace of their kin. Soon after, the mother and one of the daughters died.

The last surviving daughter, before she died six years later, had learned some English, enough to tell her protectors that at the time of her capture her tribe had numbered only thirteen. She was the last of her race, and her death marked the end of the Beothuck tribe and closed forever the blackest page of the island's history.

SOMETHING FOR EVERYONE

British Columbia advertises itself as "the ideal place in which to live, to work, to play" and from many points of view this claim is quite true. It is not surprising then to learn that a great deal of money is spent each year on catering to the needs of tourists, for tourism is the fourth largest source of income for the province.

Huge tracts of land have been set aside as parks for campers and visitors. In all, there are four national parks and 169 provincial parks that cover more than 3 400 000 ha. Over the past few years, more than three thousand campsites have been set up, each with a tent area that includes tables and benches and, in some cases, fireplaces and firewood.

A campsite, or a hotel or motel, can provide a base of operations for many forms of recreation. For the artists, whether with camera, brush, or pencil, there are innumerable chances to record the grandeur of the ages or the passing beauty of the moment. They can catch the golden glow of the setting sun above the mountains; the mountains dancing on the water; the tall trees against the driven snow; the deer delicately munching in the woods; or the coastal steamer ploughing its watery way up the long, deep inlets that mark the coast. These and a thousand other sights await the sightseer and artist alike.

There are dozens of trails to be enjoyed and for the hunters there are thousands of hectares where only game animals are to be found; for the fishermen, there are more than enough opportunities to catch trout in the inland waters or salmon in the ocean. There is so much to be found in this province of mountain, forest and ocean that there is scarcely a need that cannot be met.

THE OLDEST CITY — I

The distinction of being the oldest city in Canada must go to St. John's, the capital of the province of Newfoundland. The city also has the distinction, dubious as it may be, of being one of the most ill-fated. It took great strength and courage to overcome the ravages of war, disease and bad weather that it suffered in the past to become the bustling city that it is today.

From the beginning, even though the harbour held fishing boats from many different nations, the land itself had always been claimed by the English because of their habit of drying their catch on land instead of salting it as the other nations did. At first, the city was no more than a waterfront consisting of sheds, wharves, racks for drying fish, jumbles of barrels and casks and, here and there, a fine house owned by one of the merchant captains.

In summer, the city gave the appearance of a summer colony. Scores of vessels would enter and leave the harbour, and the rattle of anchor chains, the slap of sails, the babel of a score of languages would echo across the quiet water. Oars would flash as small boats crawled to and fro like water bugs carrying sailors, barrels of fish, and casks of fresh water. In winter, however, the scene was different. The harbour was empty and still and the only activity ashore was that of a few watchmen who waited for the fishing fleets to return in the spring.

In the two centuries that followed, the city was ravaged by death, fire, sword and disease. It survived attacks by the Dutch, by the French and by pirates. Three times the city was conquered by the French, but each time it fought back and each time it gained a little more in population, trade and prestige.

| 1 | 2 | 3 | 4 | 5 | 6 | 7 | 8 | 9 | 10 | 11 | 12 | 13 | 14 |

THE SUSQUATCH

For more than a hundred years, there has been a belief that a tribe of giant, primitive humans were living in the dark unmapped mountain areas of the Pacific northwest. Even though there have been a fair number of reports about these people, usually seen from a distance, most people refuse to believe they exist.

According to Indian legend, these wild men, the Susquatch, are the survivors of two bands of giants who almost killed each other off in battle many years ago. The finding, in recent years, of the remains of a long-extinct race of giants in Mexico has given some impetus to the belief that a few remnants of this race may have survived down to this day.

In Canada most of the sightings have been made in the mountainous area that surrounds the Upper Fraser Valley. Some people believe that these wild men live in remote caves high up in the mountains and they meet on occasion near the top of Morris Mountain where mysterious fires have been seen over the years. There are others, though, who claim that the Susquatch are too primitive to have fire as a tool and that they live only on leaves, plants and roots.

These people have been described as being anywhere from 1.8 to 4.2 m tall with a mass up to 135 kg. They are said to have wide, dark faces with very flat noses, short necks with wide sloping shoulders, and long arms that reach down to their knees. Their bodies are covered with long, dark hair tipped with silver, much like a grizzly bear. Although a large number of footprints have been found, some as much as 40 cm long, no reliable sighting of one of these people has yet been made. Until that day comes, the truth of the Susquatch will continue to remain one of the mysteries of our time.

THE OLDEST CITY — II

The weather, too, has played a major role in the misfortunes that have faced the city of St. John's. A number of bitterly cold winters added to the general misery and, in 1816, fire destroyed more than a hundred homes. A year later, some three hundred houses, wharves and food sheds burned down leaving more than 2000 people homeless. Only the arrival of a mercy ship from Boston with food and clothing averted a major famine.

In 1846, another fire raced through the city. Fanned by strong winds and fed by storage vats of seal oil, the flames consumed all but a tiny portion of the port. Some 12 000 persons were made homeless, but immediately they set up a city of tents and began to rebuild their city. The new town was barely rising when a fierce gale struck tearing away buildings, boats and wharves along the harbour. The city had scarcely recovered from this blow when a new disaster struck, this time in the form of a cholera epidemic that spread death throughout the island in 1854.

The years that followed were prosperous but, as always, good times were quickly followed by bad times. In 1892 it was another great fire. This one began with a match dropped in a stable. A good supply of water had been established in the city but by an ironic twist of fate, the water had been turned off that day to make repairs to the mains. The blaze, which roared out of control for sixteen hours, left 11 000 people without homes, and caused damage in excess of twenty million dollars. The heart of the port was a smoking ruin.

It seemed that throughout history, whenever Newfoundlanders got to their feet, they were knocked down again. However, it is also clear that nothing will stop them from getting up and trying again.

TIMED WRITINGS 7   NEWFOUNDLAND

BRITISH COLUMBIA'S NAVY — II

A cheque for slightly more than one million dollars was secretly delivered to the officer commanding the naval base by a janitor of the government buildings in Victoria. A crew of thirty-two men led by an officer headed south on a salvage tug to rendezvous with the subs which had, in the meantime, left Seattle on a "trial" run with a number of dock workers serving as crew. When the authorities realized what had happened, they sent out a search party with instructions to bring the subs back. Fortunately, the subs were lucky as a thick fog set in and they were able to evade the search ship in the darkness.

Early on the morning of August 5, the tug and subs met, the sale was completed, and the Canadian crew took over. However, because of the secrecy of the mission, not even the shore guns were aware of what had taken place so that when the two subs approached the harbour, they were reported as two German torpedo boats. When the crews of the subs realized the situation, they searched frantically and vainly for a flag. Finally they found a pillow case which they waved wildly from the tower of one of the subs. When the news of the purchase reached the ears of the public, they were jubilant.

While the people cheered, the subs went out on patrol, praying that they would not meet any enemy ships for, unknown to the public, they had no torpedoes. In fact, the subs did not even have deck guns with which to engage the enemy. The only weapons on board were rifles.

Two days after the purchase of the boats, Ottawa agreed to take them over and the "navy" became federal property. Except for one further patrol, the subs saw no action during the war and ended up, ingloriously, in a scrap heap in 1920.

PRINCE EDWARD ISLAND

Along the eastern coast of our country, swept by the winds and washed by the tides of the Atlantic Ocean, lie three provinces known to many people simply as The Maritimes. Each of the three is different from its neighbour in many ways, yet all three have much in common in their history and in their people.

The smallest of the three, in fact the smallest of all of the provinces, not only in size but also in population, is the island province of Prince Edward Island. Although this island has had a number of names since it was discovered more than four hundred years ago, to many people it is simply The Island, as though there were no other.

The best way to describe the landscape would be to say that it is a low and rolling land surrounded by fine beaches, low cliffs, and deep inlets. There are kilometres of white sand which has made this spot a favourite resort for visitors for many years. The Island has been described as a vegetable garden fenced by sandy beaches and protected by salt water; although this description is not quite accurate, it does show the important role that farming plays in the economy.

Unlike most of the other provinces, The Island has only two resources of any importance — the soil and the sea. Yet, in spite of its limited assets, the people of this small island have developed a worldwide reputation for the quality of the potatoes and seafood, such as lobsters and oysters, that they harvest each year.

The hard-working islanders have made their homeland a good place to live in, a place where there are no extremes of wealth or poverty, a place where living is pleasant.

BRITISH COLUMBIA'S NAVY — 1

In the summer of 1914, just prior to Canada's entry into the war, the naval base on Vancouver Island consisted of one old cruiser, two sloops, a tender, three launches, and a number of rowboats of various shapes and sizes. The German navy, on the other hand, had three fully armed raiders in its Pacific fleet which could have blown our navy out of the water in a few minutes.

There was a lot of concern among the people living along the coast as to how long it would be before the war would start and they would be attacked. As a result of this state of fear, many acts of panic occurred. Banks shipped gold and other securities east; citizens bought rifles to protect their homes; soldiers stood by shore guns around the clock; businesses took out war damage policies; and private cars were kept ready in case they were needed for mass evacuations.

The government of the province sent a request for more warships to Ottawa but this request was deferred. Then, on August 2, three days before our country entered the war, the government heard that there were two submarines up for sale in Seattle, 112 km to the south. A second request to Ottawa, this time to buy the subs, was again deferred so the government of the province reached into its own pocket and wrote a cheque that made it the only province since Confederation to have its own private navy.

There was, however, another problem that had to be resolved. The United States had announced a few months earlier its desire to remain neutral in the event that a war broke out and, as a result, refused to allow the sale of the subs. The only solution was to smuggle the ships out and a plan was drawn up whereby our navy would take possession outside of American waters.

NEW BRUNSWICK

New Brunswick is the most westerly of the three maritime provinces and the largest in size. It is a land of low mountains and rolling hills with rich, fertile soil. Although the eastern part of the country is more rugged, less fertile, and harsher in appearance, there is a wild beauty to this land that more than offsets its hardness.

This province, more than any other, may be described as a vast forest whose two sides are edged by fishing and farming country. As the sea is to Nova Scotia, so the forest is to New Brunswick. Almost half of all the manufacturing plants employ wood in one form or another in their products. Cutting through this huge forest are many rivers, and in the intervals, the river valleys, are located the towns and farms, the fields and the orchards. Potatoes provide the major source of income for the farmers, and their product compares favourably with that grown on The Island.

Unlike the most industrialized provinces to the west, this province still has more of its population located on farms, in tiny forest settlements, and in fishing villages than it has in the cities and towns. In many respects, it is still a pioneering land for nestled in the clearings of the interior you can find a few humble houses — the beginning of a settlement that some day may be a town — where the people still use oil lamps at night, cook on wood stoves, and pump water from a well.

Like its sister provinces, New Brunswick still relies to a large extent on the land and the sea, but this is a land rich in mineral and hydro resources that have yet to be fully developed and in which its hopes for future prosperity lie.

THE OVERLANDERS OF '62

Before the advent of the railway, most people who came to British Columbia came by sea, but a dramatic exception to this was made by a group of men and one woman who, by a daring trek over land, earned for themselves the title The Overlanders of '62.

It all began with a letter which appeared in a Toronto newspaper inviting people to join a party that would travel to the gold fields by the land route. Within a few weeks, a party was organized. The first part of the trek to Fort Garry was made by public transport — first by train, then by coach, and finally by ferry — but the next stage required them to travel on two-wheeled Red River carts drawn by oxen. The journey across the plains took nearly seven weeks to complete as the party had to contend with rivers, swamps, the weather, and hostile Indians but, if the trek across the plains had been considered difficult, it was easy compared to what lay ahead.

Beyond the fort of Edmonton, there were few if any trails, which made travel by cart impossible, so that the carts, oxen, and surplus equipment had to be traded for horses. It then took them almost a month to reach the foothills of the Rockies because of the thick brush and the swamps and rivers that had to be crossed. Although the gold fields were now only one hundred and sixty kilometres away, the mountains were impassable, and the party split up into two groups. The smaller group moved south by land, while the larger group built rafts and floated down the Fraser River. The detour added another 320 km to the journey, but both groups eventually reached their destination with the loss of only one life.

Very few ever reached the gold fields, however. The long, difficult journey of more than 4500 km became its own reward, and the great overland trek became one of the epics in the history of British Columbia.

NOVA SCOTIA

The province of Nova Scotia is a shoe-shaped mass of land jutting out into the Atlantic Ocean. This province is almost an island as it is joined to the mainland on the west by only a narrow isthmus which in places is about thirty-two kilometres wide. The most easterly part of the province is an island, Cape Breton, but it is seldom thought of as one today because of the causeway that now joins it to the mainland.

The face of this province has been deeply scored over the years by the forces of nature, and its steep edges are marked with many deep inlets, rocky coves, and ragged capes. Along the rugged coast are hundreds of lighthouses designed to warn approaching ships of the dangers that lie in wait for them. The land in the eastern part of the province is wild, mountainous, and lonely and contrasts sharply with the gently rolling hills and valleys that cover the rest of the country.

Inland, almost three-quarters of the interior is covered with dense forest from which many generations have made their living. From the harvest of millions of trees cut have come the materials needed to produce many of the wood products we use today. Although this industry has lost some of the lustre it once had in the days of wooden ships, it still plays an important role in the economy.

One of the mainstays of the province, despite the fact that so much of the land is covered with forest, is farming, which supports more of the people than does any other single industry. Because so much of the land is covered with trees, mixed farming of a modest size is the rule. Its valleys, too, have some of the finest orchards to be found anywhere, and the apples grown in the Annapolis Valley region are known throughout the world.

THE GOLD RUSH

The search for gold in the Cariboo region of British Columbia was limited in the beginning to the bars of rivers and streams. Here the prospectors panned the river gravel — that is, washed the gravel in a shallow pan — and, if they were lucky enough to find good traces of gold, they staked a claim and then began to work in earnest washing out the gold in sluice boxes rather than pans.

Latecomers were forced to move further upstream to search for gold as all the better locations in the lower regions were taken first, but it was not long before someone noticed a difference in the quality of the gold panned. On the lower reaches the gold was a fine dust, while further upriver it was more coarse. This discovery led to the conclusion, now known to be incorrect, that all the gold came from some vast mother lode far upriver. As a result, many of the prospectors moved on into the mountains in an attempt to come as close as possible to the source of the great deposits they believed were there.

Very few of the miners on any river or stream made fortunes and, more often than not, luck played a larger role than skill. Many of those who struck it rich ended with nothing as they spent or gambled their fortune away just as quickly as they made it. Thousands of others spent all they possessed, including their health, in a fruitless search. Some who came in search of gold stayed on and made a permanent home for themselves, while many others, disappointed and disillusioned, were given grubstakes to enable them to get out of the country and back home to family and friends.

Although many of the mining camps that sprang up during the frantic rush are today ghost towns, or nearly so, the fever of gold gave British Columbia the impetus it needed to grow into one of the richest and most beautiful provinces in Canada.

CHARLES DE LA TOUR — I

The unusual story of one of our first colonist families is probably one of the most interesting in our history. Charles de la Tour and his father Claude were fur traders and their base of operations was a small fort on the mainland of what is now New Brunswick. Because they were threatened by the growing strength of the Scots across the harbour at Port Royal, Charles sent his father to France for help.

On his return journey with supplies and weapons, Claude was captured by the British when his ship was sunk and he was taken prisoner back to England. Claude got along well with his captors, so well in fact that he married one of the ladies of the court. He was offered a large tract of land, and a title, in what is today Nova Scotia, if he could convert his son Charles to the British cause. Claude accepted their offer and sailed for Acadia. After a separation of more than two years, they greeted each other with much joy, until the son learned that his father wanted him to betray his country. When neither pleadings nor threats would change his son's mind, the father attacked the fort but was unsuccessful and was forced to withdraw to Port Royal.

Because of his strong stand against his father, Charles was made Lieutenant-General of Acadia. He was later given a grant of land near where the city of Saint John is located today and he established a fort there which he called Fort la Tour. Another man, called Charnisay, had meanwhile risen to a position of power and when the Scots left Port Royal, he moved in and claimed authority over all of Acadia. La Tour, however, refused to accept this new authority.

THE POTLATCH

When mention is made of British Columbia, some people think of the totem pole, a feature unique to the Indians of this province. The totem pole was almost like a coat-of-arms and represented the badge of rank or social standing of its owner.

In order to make a totem pole, a tall tree was cut down, one as free from knots and blemishes as possible, roughly prepared, and then carried to the village. On it were carved representations of the owner's ancestry, relationships, and accomplishments, either real or otherwise. The finished product was then placed in a prominent position, often in front of the house. As the raising of a totem was quite a feat in itself, it was the occasion for a great feast called a potlatch.

The potlatch played an important part in the life of the Indians before the settlers arrived, and it was held on other special occasions such as the coming of age of a son, a wedding, or the assumption of a new title by a chief. In effect, the potlatch was designed to impress the guests with the wealth, prestige, and generosity of the giver. Often a chief would save for years in order to give a potlatch and, when the great day came, presents such as canoes, ornaments, and blankets would be heaped upon the guests. Often the feast would go on for several days or until the host had nothing left to give. Though now penniless, the host was honoured and respected.

This practice was not quite as foolish as it sounds because each guest was expected, sooner or later, to hold a potlatch of his own at which time he would present to the original giver at least equal value and often twice the value of the gifts he received. Because this practice did play havoc with the economy of the Indians, it was outlawed when white people assumed control.

CHARLES DE LA TOUR — II

The two rivals, both French, faced each other across the Bay of Fundy, each feeling that he was the superior of the other. As could be expected, the rivalry between the two led to many skirmishes but with little real success. The first major attack was made by Charnisay when he led a small naval expedition against the fort. When his men were thrown back, he tried to starve the fort by blockading the harbour. La Tour, however, managed to slip away in a small boat to Boston where he was able to enlist the aid of the British. When Charnisay saw the enemy vessels approaching, he abandoned his attempt and fled back to Port Royal.

Several years later, while La Tour was away from his fort, a few of his men deserted to Charnisay. When the latter learned from them that the fort was without a leader, he attacked again, but he did not realize just what he was up against. Madame la Tour was a woman of great strength and character and she took personal command of the fort. For two months the heroic woman and the small garrison beat back every attempt to capture the fort. Finally, exhausted and out of supplies, she agreed to surrender the fort provided her men would be allowed to live. Charnisay agreed, but when he found out how small the garrison was that defeated him, he ordered every man hung, in full view of Madame la Tour. Broken hearted and alone, she died a few weeks later.

When her husband heard the news of her death and the destruction of his fort, he fled to Quebec where he stayed for five years. He returned after the death of Charnisay and married his rival's widow and, until his death, continued to play an important part in the early development of this country.

TIMED WRITINGS 12 THE MARITIMES

BRITISH COLUMBIA — II

Not too far off the coast of the province of British Columbia lie hundreds of islands, scores of which are Canadian. All are heavily wooded, some with tiny, cleared fields, nearly all with gardens, small or large. Viewed from the air, they appear as emeralds set in a silver sea, each with its own house and lake and each with its own craft moored at the wharf ready to move among the islands. By far the largest of the islands is Vancouver where Victoria, the capital of the province, is located. It is more than 400 km in length and has its own range of mountains running down the western side. The lower slopes of the island are still covered with deep forest as much of the land has yet to be settled.

Vancouver and a number of smaller islands to the north form a channel known as the Inside Passage, a safe, scenic water route which makes it possible for ships to sail to and from Alaska without being exposed to the storms and hazards of the open sea. This route has its own excitement for small craft as well. There are tidal rapids which can only be negotiated with the tide and which can carry small vessels along at two or three times their normal speed, and there are tricky currents which can sweep the lax or the unwary into rocks and whirlpools.

For all the hazards presented by such a voyage, there are more than ample compensations. Along this passage, there are long fjords and narrow inlets, some with mountains rising straight up from the water. In other places, there are weather-beaten rocks to look at and thick forests that extend down to the water's edge. Dotted along the coast are many villages with quaintly built houses, schools, and churches. For the visitor who has the time to pause and listen, many and fascinating are the tales the coastal dweller has to tell.

LOUISBOURG — 1

On the south-east shore of Cape Breton Island, where the land juts furthest into the Atlantic Ocean, there once stood one of the biggest, strongest and most expensive forts ever built. Louisbourg was ideally situated for a fort, with water on three sides and low, marshy land behind. It took more than twenty-five years to build and it cost, in modern terms, more than fifty million dollars; yet, in the two times that it was attacked, it fell both times.

The fort was an important junction for trading ships from France, the West Indies and Quebec. More important, though, to the French was the fact that it guarded the only entrance used at that time by ships entering the Gulf of St. Lawrence on their way to the interior of Canada.

Altogether, the stone and cement walls of the fort stretched for 3.2 km. The walls themselves were 3 m thick and more than 9 m in height. For protection, the fort had more than 200 cannon, some of them in the two gun batteries which were located on either side of the harbour entrance to prevent invasion by sea. On the landward side, roving bands of Indians were paid a reward for each enemy scalp they could bring in.

Within the fort itself, where the population reached as high as ten thousand at one time, was a complete town with cobbled streets. The governor's palace was the tallest building, three stories high, with space in the basement to house a garrison of troops. The palace was virtually a fort within a fort as the only entrance was by means of a drawbridge. The fort also boasted the largest hospital in the new world with 112 beds and it provided the best medical care available at that time.

BRITISH COLUMBIA — 1

The most westerly of our ten provinces, British Columbia, is a land of great expanses and exciting contrasts. There are scores of coastal islands, thick with forests, and the mainland, with more forest and bald-headed mountains, some snow-capped, which tower above the tree line. There are many rivers flowing through deep chasms, most of them too swift and treacherous to serve as means of travel, but they are rich in fish of all kinds and provide, as well, the source of much hydro power. There are also great extremes of climate, ranging from warm in the south to cold in the north and wet on the coast to dry in the interior.

It is not easy to describe this province as a single unit for its geography is varied and complex as it stretches over six hundred kilometres from Alberta to the shores of the Pacific Ocean. The province has been described as a sea of mountains, which it is, but it may come as a surprise to many to learn that the most well-known mountains, the Rockies, are but one of a series of ranges, albeit the highest and most rugged, that run roughly north-south through the province. Most of the people who live in this land think of the southern part of the province as a series of valleys separated by mountain ranges. From the summit of the Rockies on the eastern border, the land descends gently until it reaches the waters of the Pacific coast.

At first sight, a map of the land suggests the appearance of a broad, oval tray with raised sides flanking a high centre plateau. A closer look would reveal three general areas: a broad strip, about 240 km in depth, which runs from east to west and which contains the largest portion of the population; beyond this, a high central plateau, which has some of the most fertile land in the province; and, still further north, a rugged, sparsely populated mountain region.

LOUISBOURG — II

The first seige of the fort at Louisbourg took place in 1748 by an army of civilians from New England aided by a fleet of British ships. They attacked the fort in retaliation for the many attacks the French and their allies had made over the years on the colonies of New England. The army numbered about 8 000, double that of the fort itself, but the fort could not be taken. The defenders were forced to surrender after forty-six days only because their stocks of food and powder were gone. The fort was returned to the French by treaty but the reprieve proved to be short-lived.

In the ten years between the first and second attacks, the French doubled their efforts to make the fort impregnable. The total fighting force, land and sea, was increased to nearly 9 000 men and there was enough food and supplies to last for one year. Their efforts, however, proved to be in vain. In the second and last attack made in 1758, they faced a trained British army of 25 000 men and 200 warships. The fort managed to hold on for forty-nine days before it was finally overrun. To insure that the fort would never be used again, the British had it totally destroyed. The fort was so well constructed that it took engineers almost two years to raze it. Its destruction opened the gateway to Canada and marked the beginning of the end of French rule in the new world.

The fortress at Louisbourg, however, was destined to rise once again. Almost 200 years later, the first steps were taken to restore this historical site. The first phase of the project, the ten-room governor's wing has already been completed. When the project is finished, almost one-fifth of the town will have been restored, a fitting tribute to the memory of some of our first settlers.

TURTLE MOUNTAIN

High up in the Rockies of Alberta is a narrow gorge known as Crow's Nest Pass. The pass received its name from a band of Crow Indians who at one time had their main camp hidden at the top of Turtle Mountain. One of the most famous disasters of the prairies took place here and involved the small boom town of Frank.

At the turn of the present century, Frank was a rough prospecting town with a population of about one thousand, mostly miners, nestled against the steep side of Turtle Mountain. Although a small town, Frank was important to the surrounding area because of the railroad which passed through it. One night in April of 1903, a slab of limestone broke free from the mountain and started an avalanche which quickly buried the town. It was most fortunate that not more than one hundred people were killed as the avalanche demolished the community.

The slide was about 1.5 km wide, and it let loose some ninety million tonnes of rock which bounced down the mountainside tearing into the dark streets and houses far below. The avalanche shook the area for kilometres around, and the torrent of rock spread out across the valley of the pass for about 3 km with such force that it poured hundreds of metres up the mountain on the opposite side.

After the disaster the town was evacuated, but some citizens who wanted to continue living there moved to a safer site further up the mountain. However, some five years after the disaster, the mine was closed forever. Although it took thousands of men more than a month to repair the shattered railway, tonnes of broken rock still rest in the valley today, and each year tourists on guided tours ride up to the broken peak of Turtle Mountain to stand staring in awe at the boulders and rubble that still lie far below them in the pass.

SABLE ISLAND — 1

In the Atlantic Ocean, off the coast of Nova Scotia, lies a narrow crescent-shaped island called Sable Island, from "sable," the French word for sand. It is a treeless sand dune about 37 km long and 1.5 km wide. At its highest point it is not more than 24 m above sea level and the only thing that seems to hold it together is the wild grasses that grow there.

For centuries, ships have floundered on it, settlers have destroyed nature's balance by trying to farm it, and the constant buffeting by the wind and the sea has eroded it. At the time of its discovery in 1500, the island was twice its present size. A theory exists that at one time the island extended from the Grand Banks to the coast of the mainland as certain insects found there are also found only in the state of Massachusetts.

Today the main inhabitants of the island are a few families who operate the lighthouses and provide a coast guard service, a few domestic animals and more than three hundred wild horses. These horses are descendants of ones first brought over by the Spanish and which were later crossed with others brought over from the mainland. Most of them are small and stocky with short ears. They have thick fur and flowing manes, some of which are so long that they touch the ground. They are very hardy and seem impervious to the winter's storms and to the constantly blowing wind, which can gust well over 160 km an hour.

Attempts are now being made to have the island declared a national wildlife area or a national monument because it is so unique. It is the home of a type of sparrow found nowhere else and it is a sanctuary for two species of seal. Fortunately, work has already begun to repair the damage done by people in order to protect the rich, natural beauty of the island.

TIMED WRITINGS 15   THE MARITIMES

THE DINOSAURS — II

If it were not for the fact of erosion, little would be known of the animal and plant life that existed many millions of years ago. Over the ages, the ancient mud and sand which had been compressed to form shale and sandstone rock formations have been gradually worn away. In recent times, geologically speaking, the waters of the Red Deer River and its tributaries have combined with the action of rain, frost and wind to erode all the soil and vegetation. Now the badlands is a beautiful but time-worn picture of gullies, ridges, buttes and hills.

No one knows how many fossils have been lost over the years through erosion because if they are not found at the right time, they will weather out and be destroyed forever. It is also possible that there may well be thousands of fossils still buried so deeply in the sedimentary rock that they may never be discovered.

Once a fossil is located, and it may be only a single bone, or a section of a jaw, or a complete skeleton, it is outlined by using hand tools. A certain amount of the rock is left around the bone for its protection while it is being removed. If the bones are found in their natural, normal state, the remains may be mounted as they lie in the original rock. In other instances it may be decided to show the animal in a walking or standing pose, in which case an open mount is made. Here the bones are separated, cleaned, and then posed and supported by a framework of iron.

Many theories have been postulated over the years as to why the dinosaurs became extinct, but no completely satisfactory answer has yet been given. The experts simply do not know why they vanished.

SABLE ISLAND — II

Sable Island, despite its beauty, has had a grim, and sometimes sinister, history. Two large ocean currents converge near the island—the icy Labrador Current and the warm Gulf Stream—which results in fog and the island is often shrouded for weeks at a time. Estimates have been made that more than 700 ships have been wrecked on its shifting sands with the loss of thousands of lives.

The French were the first to make a serious attempt to settle the island. They placed fifty men and women on the island but they were soon forgotten by everyone when the man who sponsored them was sent to prison. It was five years before they were thought of again and when a rescue ship finally arrived, there were only eleven survivors.

As shipping across the ocean increased, so did the number of shipwrecks. Many merchants on the mainland became rich by sending search parties to the island to salvage wrecks, to help survivors, and to hunt for wild cattle, seals and walruses. The island gained an even more sinister reputation when "wreckers" set up their bases there. They would light false beacons to lure ships to the island, then loot them and murder any who survived for their possessions. Public outcry against these crimes finally led to the establishment of a life-saving station. Many lives were saved over the years that followed for, on the average, fifteen ships a year found their final resting place here.

Sable Island today is a beachcomber's delight. All kinds of flotsam and jetsam including a few coins have been found on its sands. Perhaps someday the buffeting winds and the pounding seas will combine to uncover a great treasure for someone.

THE DINOSAURS — I

The name dinosaur comes from the Greek words which mean "terrible lizard" even though, in this age, they are not considered true lizards. They are believed to have evolved from a small lizard-like reptile with a compact body and long limbs. From this early form there developed a great variety, some less than 0.6 m, others more than 2.4 m long. Today they are regarded as members of two quite distinct orders of the class Reptilia. The first order consists mainly of the flesh eaters and the second order, the plant eaters. Most of them are now extinct but a few, such as the turtle and the crocodile, still exist today and show only minor changes from their original state.

Although a few remains have been found in the soft, red sandstone cliffs that line the shores of Canada's east coast, they usually consist of the odd, water-worn bone. The largest number by far have been found in the badlands of the Red Deer River in Alberta. Of the more than four hundred species known in the world, more than sixty-five have been found in this area.

The badlands was once the bottom of an ancient shallow sea that covered most of the interior of our continent. As the animals died or were killed, sediment from the high lands flowed down, covered them, and protected them from the erosive effects of the weather. Gradually, over a period of thousands of years, they became fossilized; that is, hardened to stone. Most of the fossils that have been found in Canada have been those of animals and plants that lived and died where the mud and sand tended to accumulate — on the swamps, flood planes and deltas of the ancient sea.

| 1 | 2 | 3 | 4 | 5 | 6 | 7 | 8 | 9 | 10 | 11 | 12 | 13 | 14 |

THE ACADIANS I

Between the time the French conceded Acadia and the time they gave up all claims to land in what is today Canada, there occurred one of the most tragic events in the long history of the Maritimes. It concerned the Acadians, the French farmers and fishermen who remained in their homeland even though it had been turned over to the British.

These people, more concerned with their own way of life than with politics, continued to live quietly as they had been doing for years. Although they were required by law to take an oath of allegiance to the new rule, most of them did not bother, and the British took no action to see that the order was enforced.

However, the war between the two powers continued and, as it grew more intense, a few of the British settlers expressed fears over the loyalty of these people. The French group argued that, if not wholly in favour of the new rule, they were at least neutral. In spite of their protests, the cry raised was loud enough that the governor of the colony ruled that they be deported.

In all, about six thousand Acadians were rounded up and loaded onto ships. Attempts were made to keep families together but, in many cases, parents were separated from their children and wives from their husbands. They were only allowed to take with them those items that they could carry—all other goods such as tools and livestock had to be left behind. The ships took them south to a number of ports in what was then the American colonies, where they were left to find new lives for themselves. Their homes were then burned to the ground, and their cattle and grain taken to cover the costs of deporting them.

1 | 2 | 3 | 4 | 5 | 6 | 7 | 8 | 9 | 10 | 11 | 12 | 13 | 14

THE NORTHWEST REBELLION — II

Because they were afraid that their homes and their freedom would be lost, the Metis named Louis Riel to act as their leader. Riel tried to ensure that the region would govern itself, and in many ways he worked within the law as he understood it, but his part in the trial and execution of a young surveyor angered the people in the east and aroused bitter hatred against Riel. A police force was sent west to restore order but before they arrived, Riel fled and went into hiding.

During the years that followed, as the new railway moved across the plains, the Metis found that the area in which they were free to live and hunt was rapidly becoming smaller. So, too, were the number of buffalo to be found. The Metis felt that some action had to be taken before their situation became desperate so, in 1884, they asked Riel to return as their leader. At first Riel had the support of most of the population as they believed he would work on their behalf; however, when his petitions did not bring the immediate results he had hoped for, Riel turned to force and violence and lost much of his support. For a time the north was threatened with war as the rebels raided settlements, burned houses and killed innocent people. Troops were sent from the east and, after a series of battles, defeated the rebels. Riel surrendered, was tried and convicted for treason, and hung.

His death led to great differences in opinion between the two founding races and what had begun as a struggle between an old way of life and a new way of life ended in much bitterness towards other races and religions. If only the government had listened to the cry of the Metis and helped them adjust to a new life, much of the trouble and strife might have been avoided.

THE ACADIANS II

At the time the Acadians were deported to the colonies in the south, no notice was given in many cases of their coming. Once ashore, few of them had places to stay; fewer still had money enough to feed themselves, let alone begin a new life. As a result, many died of hunger and exposure.

Not all of the people were taken to distant and strange lands. Some, forewarned of what was to come, fled into the dense forests that covered so much of the country and made new homes, while others worked their way west into French-held territory. Large numbers of those deported found their way to the large French colony around New Orleans where their descendants still live today.

After peace had been declared at Quebec in 1763, when the French gave up all their claims to land in what is today Canada, small groups of Acadians drifted back to their native land. They could not return to their homes, for they had been burned, or even to their lands, which had been given to new settlers, but they did manage to find places for themselves and once more renewed their former ways of life.

The plight of the Acadians will always be remembered as long as people continue to read the well-known poem Evangeline. Longfellow, in moving, stately verse, tells of the love of Evangeline, daughter of a farmer, for Gabriel, son of a blacksmith, and how she devoted her whole life to looking for him after they had become separated while being deported. It is such a beautiful story that the heroine has been adopted as the symbol of Acadian womanhood, and a statue in her honour may be found today in front of the chapel in Grand Pré, Nova Scotia.

THE NORTHWEST REBELLION — I

By the year 1860 there were close to 12 000 people living on the prairies. Almost half of these were Metis, a loosely-knit group of people whose ancestry was a mixture of French and Indian. For a good many years they had run their own affairs and they considered themselves as a free and sovereign people but trouble began when the new settlers from the east moved in. These new people, with little understanding of the kind of free society that existed in the west, wanted the whole region to join the new nation of Canada. As a result of this, and other differences, a bitter dispute arose between the old and the new, not between races or religions, but these factors came to play a major role as the two sides clashed.

When the government in Ottawa bought all of the western lands from the Hudson's Bay Company in 1869, most of the people were happy with the transfer that united the plains with the rest of the new nation. There were others, however, especially the Metis, who were both resentful and fearful. Many of them felt that the influx of new settlers, the increase in farming, the rumours of a new railway which would be built, and the growing number of settlements that had sprung up already doomed the free and easy life of the buffalo-hunting Indians and Metis.

The government erred when it failed to reassure the Metis that their rights would be protected. In the years that followed, this failure, added to the natural fears of the Metis, and the pride in the homes that they had made for themselves after years of struggle, led to a bitter and violent clash that had far-reaching effects on our country.

THE OAK ISLAND MYSTERY — 1

Everybody loves a mystery, and the mystery that exists on a small island off the coast of Nova Scotia has no equal. At one time, pirates roamed the area and, as a result, there are untold numbers of stories of buried treasure. Ever since the island was discovered in 1795, people have been trying to discover what lies at the bottom of a shaft that has come to be known as "the money pit."

Many millions of dollars have been spent over the years in an attempt to answer this question. Despite more than twenty attempts, each of which seemed to provide some tantalizing clue, the only things of real value that have been brought up are three links of gold chain and a scrap of parchment. No one has yet reached the bottom of the pit for each time that success seemed close, water flooded the shaft and drowned the hopes of the searchers. Many experts feel that all the searchers over the years may have shifted the unknown treasure hundreds of metres from its original position.

The first searchers, three teen-age boys, began their efforts after one of the boys, out hunting for game on the uninhabited island, discovered an odd depression at one end of the island. Directly above the depression, on a sawed-off tree limb, hung a ship's block and tackle. The boys dug to a depth of 9 m and at each 3 m level they found a platform of aged oak logs. They had to abandon their efforts, however, as the task was too great for the simple tools they had. The people on the mainland refused to help because they believed that the island was inhabited by the ghosts of two fishermen who disappeared there many years ago when they went to investigate some strange lights they had seen on the island.

THE REDCOAT

When the Royal Canadian Mounted Police force was first established in 1873 under the name the North West Mounted Police, the one item of clothing that was thought to be essential was the scarlet tunic. To the Indians, the "redcoat" of the British cavalry meant trust and respect because they had always been treated fairly by them. Even though parts of the uniform have changed over the years, the one item that remains as a link to the original force is the "redcoat". Today, however, the tunic is worn only on special occasions or during the Musical Ride.

The full ceremonial dress of the Force today, in addition to the scarlet tunic, consists of blue-black breeches with the wide, yellow stripe of the cavalry down the side seam and long, brown riding boots with box spurs. The broad-brimmed felt hat is a military version of the common cowboy hat that was worn in the west, and which has proved to be useful as a protection against the elements.

For most people, the only chance they have of seeing the full dress uniform is during a performance of the Musical Ride. The Ride was derived from a cavalry drill that was part of the basic training of the Force in the early days and it consists of 32 men on black horses doing intricate drill to music. This performance proved to be so popular with the public that by 1904 it was performed at fairs and exhibitions all over the west. Today the Ride is known all over the world, and many people who know little about our country are familiar with the Mounted Police and its uniform. To many, the "redcoat" is still looked upon as the epitome of honesty, justice and fair play.

THE OAK ISLAND MYSTERY — II

Later searchers eventually found that the mysterious oak tiers were placed 3 m apart to a depth of 27 m. Not more than 3 m further down, a crowbar struck a solid mass which searchers felt was the treasure chest but, by next morning, they returned to find the shaft covered in 18 m of water. It was many years later before searchers discovered that someone had built an ingenious system of flood tunnels to protect whatever they had hidden there.

Drill rigs were brought in to try and locate the flood tunnels as well as to discover the exact position of the treasure. One drill core showed evidence of 17.5 cm of cement, 12.5 cm of oak, 70 cm of small metal pieces, then more oak and cement. Another drill struck solid iron which it could not penetrate and brought up a scrap of parchment bearing a few odd letters written in India ink with a quill pen. In 1967, a drill core brought up bits of wood and fragments of china from a depth of over 60 m and, from still another, a piece of brass which experts estimate was several hundred years old.

Then there are the numerous little pieces in the puzzle which have not yet been fitted in: the stone with the date 1704 chiselled in it; the notched logs with the Roman numeral markings, the oak pegs and iron nails; and the mysterious wooden box. The experts are baffled. Someone went to great lengths to build flood tunnels to protect that something, and all clues indicate that it was done prior to 1709. Despite modern technology and equipment, "the money pit" continues to remain a mystery.

THE NORTH WEST MOUNTED POLICE II

The largest group of Indians to come north at one time was the Sioux, more than six thousand in all, who fled the American west following the famous battle at the Little Big Horn. They had repaid violence with violence, and they had no way of guessing what fate awaited them in Canada. At the border, to their surprise, they were met by a group of ten Mounties, rather than the large force of armed men that they expected. This action showed the Sioux not only the courage of the redcoats, but also the respect for the law which they required. The Sioux were allowed to stay in Canada only after they agreed to obey the laws of this land. Many times in the history of the force, the Mounties were called upon to act in a similar manner to maintain law and order.

The members of this force were looked upon more as friends than as policemen. Often the Mountie was the only outside contact a lonely white settler had for many months at a time for, no matter how isolated a settler family might be, they could expect to receive a visit from their Mountie on patrol every few weeks. He travelled by horse, dogsled, or snowshoe, bringing the latest news from the outside, carrying parcels and mail, helping to treat the sick or injured; he shoed horses, repaired traps, told settlers where game might be plentiful and, in general, helped in any way he could to make their lives more pleasant.

Just as he brought news to the lonely farms and settlements, so he received news of what was happening along the route of his patrol. Each member of the force kept written records of his visits and his duties, and this information proved to be valuable in preventing lawlessness from gaining a foothold in the west. The fair but firm action of this police force earned them the title "The Friendly Force."

THE BLUENOSE — I

On the reverse side of all Canadian dimes you will see the beautiful trim lines of a two-masted schooner that for a period of seventeen years won for Canada the reputation of excellence in racing. It was called the Bluenose, the nickname American fishermen gave to all people who lived in Nova Scotia, and from its very first race in 1921 was virtually unbeatable.

There has always been a rivalry between the fishermen of New England and those of Nova Scotia as to which side had the fastest boats, and contests were often held whenever they met at sea. The Americans usually won as the Canadian boats were built more for capacity than speed. In the first sponsored race between the top fishing boats of both countries in 1920, the United States boat won so handily that it caused great embarrassment to the proud people of Nova Scotia. Not to be outdone, they built a new fishing schooner with trimmer, sleeker lines, similar to those of a yacht. It was deep-bellied and spoon-bowed with a very high bow that caused many an old fisherman to remark that it would never be able to win.

But the Bluenose did, and in 1921 won the championship it was never to lose. Oddly enough, it was the great bow that allowed Bluenose to win because it enabled the boat to ride easily over the whitecaps that caused other boats to shudder under the impact of the waves crashing down on the decks.

In the nine years that followed, the Bluenose was challenged twelve times and each time won handily. The first and only loss came in 1930 when it lost two of three races to an American boat. The loss would never have happened except for a human error on the part of the captain. The Bluenose came back the next year and easily beat the same boat in two straight races.

TIMED WRITINGS 21   THE MARITIMES

THE NORTH WEST MOUNTED POLICE I

Aside from a few disputes and the odd skirmish, the Riel Rebellion was the only real disturbance to mar the otherwise peaceful settlement of our west. In sharp contrast, the history of the American west was filled with accounts of many battles, and settlement came only after thousands of red and white men had been killed. Even after the land was settled, there was much violence and lawlessness which made life difficult for the settlers. Indian wars, outlaws, and holdups have long provided data for books and films but, in fact, the violence was a real tragedy for all concerned. The same problems might just as easily have been faced in our country except for a small group of dedicated men — the North West Mounted Police.

For many years after it was first set up in 1873, the force numbered only three hundred men, but they carried out their task of keeping peace and order with such courage and fairness that they soon won the respect of all people, red and white. The major purpose of the force was the care and protection of all the people, red as well as white, and they were prepared to defend the innocent and punish the guilty no matter what their race or colour.

The Indians found over the years that the Mounties, as they came to be known, were not afraid to ride alone into a camp of armed red men just to recover a single horse, and yet they were just as quick to defend them from abuse or cheating by the whites. The red coat of their uniforms became respected by the Indians for its fair and impartial treatment. Even more important, by their patience and understanding the men of the Mounted were able to leave the Indian with his self-respect, a most important possession which was in danger of being lost.

THE BLUENOSE — II

Despite its successes in racing, the Bluenose was first and foremost a fishing schooner and when it was not racing it earned good profits for its crew and owners. The Bluenose captured the imagination of people throughout the world and was shown at the world fair in Chicago in 1933 and at the silver jubilee of George V in England in 1935. Bluenose was the last of the great wooden sailing ships and its days were numbered as squat but efficient diesel trawlers began to appear more and more on the fishing banks.

The Bluenose ran its last race in 1938—the year it was given permanent possession of the Fishermen's Cup—against the same boat it had defeated seven years earlier. By now, though, Bluenose was time-worn and weary yet it managed to win two of the first three races. It would have won the fourth, too, except that the backstays parted in a strong wind. In the fifth and deciding race, with thousands watching on shore and millions listening on radio, the Bluenose jumped into an early lead and led all the way. However, with victory in sight, the staysail halyard block gave away and the challenger came storming up. There was no time for repairs, only hope, and somehow Bluenose managed to hang on and win by a scant three minutes to claim its final victory.

When the captain of the ship, Angus Walters, retired from the sea in 1939, he wanted the province to preserve the boat as a monument but, with war approaching, the public's attention shifted and the Bluenose was all but forgotten. The captain tried to keep the boat but the personal expense involved was too much and it had to be sold. The Bluenose ended its glorious career rather sadly, four years later and far from home, on a reef off the Caribbean island of Haiti.

A STRANGE CROP

Our three Prairie provinces are well known throughout the world for the high quality of wheat they produce and they have well earned the nickname "bread basket of the world", but the first cash crop produced in this area was quite unique—buffalo bones.

All across the land lay the remains of buffalo that had fallen over the years to the lances and arrows of the Indians and to the bullets of the Metis and the white hunters, their bones bleached under the sun. The dried bones were used for bleaching or whitening sugar and as a fertilizer. The demand was so great, particularly in the United States, that not only did the people profit from this "crop" but also the railways, to whom any prosperity meant greater profits.

Fire was used in many cases so that the white bones would stand out more clearly against the stubble which remained. At first the bones were carried out of the region by the famous Red River cart, but as the industry proved to be so profitable, most of the bones were collected and piled along the railway tracks. In some places the bones numbered in the millions. They were piled as high as boxcars and, in some cases, were several city blocks long. Long trains of open boxcars then took the bones to the south and east for refining.

This short-lived industry of the 1890s had to die as there was a limit to the supply of bones. The great herds of buffalo which once roamed over the plains became virtually extinct. Humans, however, were able to reap this one last benefit from a great animal which had already supplied them with so much.

| 1 | 2 | 3 | 4 | 5 | 6 | 7 | 8 | 9 | 10 | 11 | 12 | 13 | 14 |

SUNKEN TREASURE

A good many boys and girls, and possibly even a few adults, have dreamed of the day when they would find sunken treasure. Some people may have probably wished, also, that they lived in the West Indies where, it seems, wrecks filled with gold, silver and jewels are found almost every year.

Most people, however, are not aware that at the bottom of some of our own water routes lie the wrecks of an untold number of ships, many of them filled with treasures of their own. Records show that more than seven hundred ships have been destroyed on the reefs and spits of Sable Island alone and that another six hundred or more lie off the southern coast of Newfoundland.

In the Great Lakes, too, there are at least thirty known wrecks whose final resting places have been closely pinpointed. At least thirteen of these wrecks are found in Lake Erie, most near the eastern end. They were probably destroyed by the sudden storms that often tear with little or no warning across this shallow-bottomed lake.

The last find, one of the largest in Canada, was made in 1966 when a team of treasure hunters found part of the payroll of the French ship Le Chameau which sunk in 1725 off the reefs of Fort Louisbourg in Nova Scotia. The divers discovered almost nine thousand gold and silver coins which were first valued at more than $700 000, but which are now estimated to be worth only $25 000. It seems that the more you find, the less each piece is worth because it is rarity that causes prices to be high. The truth behind looking for sunken treasure is that the search can be long and costly and is seldom rewarding. As of this writing, the courts still have not yet decided who has the rights of ownership to the treasure found in 1966.

| 1 | 2 | 3 | 4 | 5 | 6 | 7 | 8 | 9 | 10 | 11 | 12 | 13 | 14 |

TIMED WRITINGS 23 — THE MARITIMES

THE RED RIVER CART

Before the days of water and train travel on the prairies, one of the earliest vehicles used, one that is still remembered by many people today through stories and motion pictures, was the Red River cart. This cart is the Canadian counterpart of the covered wagon which was made famous in the settling of the American west.

The Red River cart looked much like a huge basket set between two large wheels. This cart was quite unique because not one fragment of metal was used in its construction. The wooden wheels had tires made of buffalo hide which was soaked and beaten until it was soft and moist. The hide was then fastened to the rims of the wheels and left to dry. When it hardened, the tires were tough and durable, able to withstand the severe treatment they received on the rough wilderness roads.

Up until the middle of the 19th century, it was fairly common to see freight trains consisting of a hundred or more of these carts, each pulled by a single ox and manned by a driver. The longest train on record is said to have consisted of more than five hundred carts and oxen. Because of the large number of carts that were needed, the first factory on the prairies was set up to meet the demand for these vehicles.

In time, however, these carts were replaced by big sturdy freight wagons with steel axles. Three of these wagons were usually attached together and were pulled by a team of from six to twelve oxen hitched in pairs. A group of these three-wagon outfits was called a bull-train, and each was capable of carrying many hundreds of tonnes of food and supplies across the plains. As 16 km a day was considered good travelling time, the business of moving cargo and receiving supplies en route was very slow and tedious.

QUEBEC

Quebec is the largest in size by far of all the provinces, with almost three-quarters of its land mass bounded by water. This is not a soft country. In many places it is stern, even forbidding.

This is the land of the Canadian Shield, a once mighty upthrust of granite that was born billions of years ago when the earth was still in its infancy. The Shield alone covers more than ninety per cent of the total area, and on its breast are mountains ranging up to several thousand metres in height. There is, in addition, a second, much smaller range which runs roughly north-south along the eastern edge of the province. The Shield, at first, was a great obstacle to travel and expansion but once conquered was found to be one of the richest treasure houses of minerals and hydro power ever discovered and, as yet, it is barely touched.

In the northern regions, beyond the mountain ranges, is the wilderness tableland where the forests gradually dwindle into a vast area of rocks, turbulent rivers, coastal barrens and tundra, with little, if any, tree cover. Here one can find thousands of shallow lakes that have been scooped out of the rock by eons of time and weather. Some people call this region bleak; to others, it is a land of quiet, dark beauty.

In the south, between the two mountain ranges, lies the softly rolling pastoral land where the greatest number of people live. Because of its easy access to the sea and the fertility of its soil, it is the oldest settled area in the province. In this broad trench dug out over the ages by the outpouring of rivers to the sea are located the farms and the quaint villages, the towns and the noisy, bustling cities.

THE SELKIRK SETTLEMENT

    The Prairies, like the rest of our country, developed very slowly in the beginning as the first white people on the plains were interested only in making a profit from furs and hides. The first real effort at settlement was made by a Scottish landowner named Selkirk. When it became clear to Lord Selkirk that the land he owned was not suitable for farming, he tried to find ways to help those tenants who had nowhere else to go. He spent a great deal of time and money helping many of them to relocate on the Canadian prairies.

    The immigrants were offered free grants of land and, if they were unable to pay, free transportation. Men who agreed to sign up as labourers in the new colony were given three-year contracts and a bonus of forty hectares of land at the end of their service. Only by such inducements was Selkirk able to convince the poor tenants to abandon their worthless farms and travel a long and hazardous journey to a new and unknown country.

    Life was far from easy for the first settlers who faced hunger as the most important problem. The first crops planted were killed by an early frost, but the settlers soon discovered, as the Indians had hundred of years earlier, that the movement of the buffalo dictated their actions.

    There were many disputes, some burnings and a near war with the traders and trappers before Selkirk was able to come over and take charge of the colony. Under his direction, churches were planned, roads built and new supplies of poultry, swine, cattle and seed were brought in. It was this determination to stay and make a new home that opened the land for others to follow.

1 | 2 | 3 | 4 | 5 | 6 | 7 | 8 | 9 | 10 | 11 | 12 | 13 | 14

TIMED WRITINGS 53   THE PRAIRIES

HOCHELAGA

Because of its location on the St. Lawrence River, it is no accident that Montreal, the largest city in Canada and the second largest French-speaking city in the world, is one of the great cities of the world. Montreal has always had a distinctive flavour but, since the end of the last war, it has become even more so — a gourmet's delight and a centre of culture. However, even before the explorers arrived, Hochelaga, as Montreal was first known, was one of the largest permanent Indian settlements in the new world.

According to the log of one of the first men to explore our continent, Cartier, he and his men were greeted by more than a thousand men, women and children when they reached Hochelaga for the first time. The natives assembled in a group and danced round and round raising a din of merriment. They brought the explorers fish and coarse bread which they tossed into the boats so that the food seemed to be coming from the sky.

Cartier was so moved by their greeting that he landed with a party of men. No sooner were they on the ground before everyone gathered around them and made a tremendous fuss. They brought the women and children so that the captain might touch them, and his men likewise, making a great party of it all. The captain, in return for their good will, gave them trinkets and knives. After the reception, the party returned to the boats, while the Indians remained on shore making fires and dancing and singing well into the night.

This was an eerie scene for a small party of white men in the heart of the unknown, such a distance from the familiar hearths of France; a bit frightening, probably, even for brave men, but what an exciting welcome to a new land.

OPENING THE WEST — II

The short-sighted policy of the governor changed the future of the West. Radisson and Groseilliers travelled to France to protest the treatment they had received and to convince the King of the importance of their discovery. They were given no help there but, firm in their belief about the riches of the north, they went to England to plead their case. Here their luck was better and two ships were sent to the Bay. They returned with such a load of furs that all doubts about the wealth of the North were dispelled.

A charter was issued in 1670 to "The Governors and Company of Adventurers of England trading into Hudson's Bay." This was the founding of the Hudson's Bay Company which, by its charter, was given not only a monopoly on the fur trade in the West, but the ownership of all the lands drained by the rivers which flow into the Bay. Some of these rivers flowed from the Rockies which meant, in effect, that the charter gave all of the West to the Company. The land was given the name Rupert's land after the man who financed the first venture.

At first there was little exploration of the huge territory because the traders stayed close to home and waited for the Indians to bring their furs to the trading post. It was not until after rival traders came in from the east that the Company started to build its posts. As it moved inland, it found that each new post brought new and increasing numbers of Indians and, with their furs, came stories of other tribes and new hunting grounds. The story of the Company is a story of trading posts that eventually reached the shores of the Pacific Ocean.

NEW FRANCE I

Although the Vikings appear to be the first to discover and land on our shores, the rest of the world at that time was sleeping through a period known as the Dark Ages and knew nothing, or cared very little, about a new land to the west. Almost five hundred years were to pass before Europe slowly emerged into a more enlightened age, an era of discovery, not for the sake of adventure or even knowledge, but for trade and profit. Princes and merchants turned their eyes westward and sent their ships in the hope of finding new and faster routes to the far east.

Much of the credit given to the explorers for their courage in venturing into the unknown rightfully belongs to the simple fishermen, for it was they who first travelled further afield with each voyage to profit from the public demand for fish and other treasures of the sea. It must be remembered that meat was not the staple it is today and that there were innumerable feast days that called for fish only. It was from these fishermen that many explorers obtained the maps and charts that showed the best sailing routes, and it was from these same people that they learned much about the winds, currents, and weather of the seas to the west.

Cartier, a former fisherman, wrote the first chapter in the exploration of our world by the French. His experience was such that he was given a royal commission to discover certain islands and countries where there would be found gold and other riches. In all, he made three less than profitable journeys to our world, and it was many years before anyone else dared to battle with scurvy or face the bitter cold of our winters, but Cartier was the first to explore our land and he opened the door for those that were to follow in the years to come.

OPENING THE WEST — I

Although Hudson Bay was first discovered in 1610 and was visited on other occasions by ships searching for the fabled Northwest Passage as a shorter route to China, the credit for opening up the West has to be given to Pierre Radisson and Chouart des Groseilliers. They were men who knew and loved the Northwest. They travelled deep into the dense northern forests; they traded with the Indians, they explored the land. They were the first to sense the hidden wealth of fur.

These two men, the most famous of the "coureurs de bois," first travelled to the unknown lands of the Northwest in the 1650s. After a silence of two years, the people of Quebec were surprised to see a fleet of fifty canoes arrive at the city carrying a huge cargo of furs. The road to the West was opened and, in the years following, many more ventures into the vastness of the unknown West were made by these and other men of the woods.

It is not clear how far they travelled on the trip which had such far-reaching consequences, but it is known that they got as far as the edge of the Great Lakes and learned, through observation and conversation, that the country to the west must be on the watershed of Hudson Bay. They collected stories about Indian travel to the great water to the north. They were able to return not only with a valuable cargo, but with the exciting knowledge that, in the future, fur trading could centre directly on the Bay itself. This was especially good news because the more valuable fur country was in the north and the Bay was much nearer to open sea and the route to Europe.

The governor of Quebec, however, did not share in their enthusiasm. He seized their furs on the grounds that they had not obtained his permission and were, therefore, trading without a licence.

NEW FRANCE II

The second chapter in the history of our country was written by Champlain nearly fifty years after Cartier had failed in his search to find the riches of our land. Champlain, from the time he first arrived in this country in 1603 until his death thirty-two years later, did more to develop a French colony here than did any other individual. He was the first to explore a large portion of the continent, as well as train other young men in the art. He played a major role in founding the first permanent colony in what is now Quebec, and it was he who formed an alliance with the local Indians which opened up the area for settlement.

For more than one hundred years following his death, New France, as it was called, grew slowly. Settlers were brought in to clear and farm the land and, as the towns grew, schools and churches were built. Many of the more hardy settlers moved deep into the forests of the interior to farm, to trap, or to trade in the forts and outposts that had sprung up. As the colony prospered, more soldiers were sent over to guard their welfare and more clerks to make laws and collect taxes. Yet, despite the small but steady flow of people that came to the new land, growth of the colony was more dependent on the high birth rate than on immigration.

As the settlers moved further west, they came into contact more and more with the English and their allies, the Iroquois, who were pushing north and west. These contacts frequently resulted in conflicts and even, in some cases, massacres. Dispute over the land became more intense with each passing year and led, finally, to war being declared between the two powers. The struggle which lasted off and on for seven years was decided once and for all when the French were defeated at the battle of Quebec.

FROM TRAVOIS TO THE HORSE

At the time the first Indian ranged the plains, the horse was not even known. The closest thing to transportation which he possessed was the travois, a framework of wood which was harnessed to a dog. The travois was made by tying a long, thin pole to each side of a dog just between his shoulders and attaching a rack between the poles from his tail to the end of the wood. The poles dragged on the ground and, with a load of goods tied securely to the rack, the dog could travel for a long way without tiring.

With the coming of the horse early in the 18th century, and then later, firearms, the life and structure of the tribe changed quite markedly. The horse, which had been introduced years earlier on the continent by the Spanish, eventually found its way north, brought by traders who knew their value or by herds that simply wandered up from the south. Isolated, fearful tribes of foot-hunters, who could travel neither far nor fast, suddenly found themselves mobile.

The four tribes of the plains, who met only occasionally in the past, now came into more frequent meetings with each other, and great rivalry grew up between them. Each wanted to hunt the buffalo farther afield, faster, and with greater efficiency than the others, and the desire to rule the richest lands led to the development of an elaborate system of tribal warfare which led, in turn, to many changes being made in the structure and organization of each tribe.

Within the tribes, the horse became the most valuable form of currency, as well as a status symbol. Many Indians traded their precious buffalo hides for horses, if they could get them, or else they made raids on the settlers or on other tribes in order to obtain them. In a very short time, the wealth and prestige of an Indian came to be measured in terms of the number of horses he owned.

JEAN TALON, INTENDANT — I

Before 1661, the colony of New France was under private charter to a company whose only interest was to make money in the fur trade. Although responsible for the development and settlement of the land, the company, in practice, did very little. It was not until after the King of France decided to develop the colony that growth began to take place. In the years that followed, many able men and some not so able were sent over to administer the colony. The first and probably the most energetic and successful was a man named Jean Talon. As Intendant he was the business administrator and in the two short periods that he spent in the new world, he did much to make the colony self-sufficient.

Talon was a man of great insight and ability. He had horses, cattle and sheep brought in for the settlers. He imported looms and insisted that the women learn to spin and weave the wool from their own sheep. In order to encourage them to grow hemp and flax, he supplied the seed. From the hemp, bags and cloth were made; from the flax, linen was spun. He established a tannery to utilize the hides of the animals and this led, in turn, to the manufacture of shoes and other leather goods. History has it that Talon, before he returned to France, was able to report: "I am now clothed from head to foot with home-made articles."

In order to become self-supporting, the colony had to develop its own resources which it could trade for the goods it needed. A shipyard was built and the cod and seal industries were encouraged to expand. Trade with the West Indies was increased. The lumber and fish of Canada were traded for rum and sugar which was then sold to the mother country in order to bring in the manufactured articles needed by the colonists.

THE PRAIRIE INDIANS

The first people on the Prairies were the Indians, but no one knows exactly how many of these people lived there. It is known that there were four major tribes and that they all depended upon the land for their existence. The tribes were nomads who ranged from place to place following the large buffalo herds as they went in search of better feeding grounds. Before the horse was introduced in the 18th century, movement of the tribes was quite slow and limited in range as they travelled only by foot taking all their possessions with them as they went.

Their whole economy was based on one staple, the buffalo, so that most of their time and energy was spent in searching for them. The buffalo could have a mass of a tonne, and the meat from just one of these creatures was usually enough to sustain a number of families for a long period of time. So vital was this animal that little of the carcass was ever wasted. The hides or skins were used to provide clothing and shelter, as well as aids in travelling from one place to another. Plains Indians, unlike their brothers of the forest, used light boats made from skins that were stretched over a circular framework of willow branches. This gave them the appearance of large baskets. The hide of the cow buffalo was used to make moccasins and light leather clothing, while the heavier hide of the bull was used to make winter clothing and blankets, as well as serving as walls for their tipis.

Although the Indian was usually free to come and go as he wished, regulations that governed a tribe during the hunt were quite strict. Severe punishment was meted out to anyone who broke a rule, disobeyed an order, or frightened one of the animals, even by accident. The mere sight or sign of a human was enough to terrify these beasts, and the whole herd would run far and long to escape.

JEAN TALON, INTENDANT — II

Jean Talon was also a man of considerable wisdom. He realized that if the colony were to grow and prosper, it would need more people. The obvious way to expand was to ask the King to send more settlers but many, fearful of the long sea voyage and the stories of cold winters and Indian savagery, were content to remain at home.

Talon then tried to encourage growth from within the colony itself. Parents were advised that their sons should be married before they reached the age of twenty; daughters, before the age of sixteen. Parents who objected to the request were taken to court and fined—twice a year if necessary. The men who did get married were given a gift of money to enable them to start a new life; those who did not were denied permission to hunt in the forests.

Talon then tried a new experiment. Realizing that most pioneer settlements contained more men than women, Talon asked the King to send him women to become the wives of the bachelors. The women, called "daughters of the King," were carefully chosen and were, for the most part, country women with limited prospects at home. The women came over in lots of a hundred or more under supervision and they were taken to a convent where they could be interviewed by the bachelors. They were in no way forced to marry someone they did not like. They, in turn, could question the men they were interested in and find out their habits and resources. As soon as a couple agreed to get married, the wedding took place right away. As a gift from the Crown, the new couple were given food, livestock and a gift of money. The experiment was so successful that Talon was able to report that in one year alone almost 700 babies had been baptized.

THE PRAIRIES II

The history of the Prairies began more than a million years ago when the great ice fields began to retreat slowly northward. In their wake the land warmed, and the melting ice formed huge inland lakes that for eons covered so much of the land that today produces most of our wheat. Water carrying deposits of silt, clay, and sand, and ice blocks clogged with earth, flowed into the lakes and over a period of time gradually filled them in. Ages before our history began in this country, the shallow lakes had dried out and the heavy, black soil lay waiting for the plow and the hoe to seek out its riches.

The Canadian Shield covers the largest portion of the land we call the Prairies, much as it does the rest of Canada. The ice-caps of long ago had crushed the soft rocks on the surface of the higher lands, deposited the debris in the valleys, and scoured the hard rocks, leaving behind only rounded granite stubs alternating on the face of the land with swamp and muskeg. Untold numbers of short, turbulent rivers and quiet, sparkling lakes dot the Shield which is still frontier land in many respects, passable by water only and used mainly by trappers, traders, and Indians. Beneath the cold, rugged terrain, buried deep below the surface, lies much of the mineral wealth of the Prairies.

The rest of the area, the land between the vast wheat fields and the bare rock of the north, is covered in a dark, green forest which appears to anyone looking to be holding the Shield from moving further south. Here may be found many species of trees, such as aspen, poplar, spruce, and jackpine, as well as the occasional small farm.

| 1 | 2 | 3 | 4 | 5 | 6 | 7 | 8 | 9 | 10 | 11 | 12 | 13 | 14 |

THE SEIGNIORY — I

It was logical that when land was allotted to the settlers in New France that it would be based on the old feudal system used in France. Under this system the King owned all the land, but he granted large areas to the most powerful nobles who supported him. They in turn would grant smaller parcels to the lesser nobles. The lesser nobles would then grant small sections to the peasants who farmed the land. This whole system of land ownership was designed so that small communities could produce the food needed to feed themselves and their lords.

In New France, large tracts of land were granted to anyone willing to try life in the new colony. A man who held a grant of land was called a seignior and his land was called his seigniory. He in turn was expected to find tenants, called habitants, who were willing to work the land. As seignior he had certain duties and responsibilities. He had to give the governor a map outlining the boundaries of his grant and he had to prepare a census listing the number of people on it, the number and type of farm animals he had, the type of crops he was growing, and how much land he had cleared. It was his duty to see that the tenants cleared and tilled a satisfactory amount of land annually. Both parties were required to give military service, if needed, and to build roads.

By the terms of his grant, the seignior was required to build a grist mill. The habitants were obliged to use it and to give the seignior some of their flour in payment. The mills were usually constructed of stone and in cases of attack, the families living on a seigniory could take refuge there. The seignior was also responsible for organizing the habitants to defend the settlement against attack.

THE PRAIRIES I

The very name, the Prairies, calls to mind huge vistas of unending plains or flat, wide-open spaces which like the ocean stretch as far as the eye can see. The wheatlands do look like a broad, golden ocean when the winds turn the sunny fields into ebbing and flowing waves of billions of shiny, yellow wheat heads, but the name is a little misleading. Less than one-third of the total land of the three provinces that make up what is known as the Prairies is true flat land even though it stretches over twelve hundred kilometres from east to west.

The rest of the land is a vivid contrast of grassland and muskeg, of steep cliffs and rolling hills, of stubby rocks and quiet lakes, of brown water and rushing rapids, of inviting green and repelling grey, of towering forest and stunted growth. Above the colours and the contrasts of the land extend the symbols of the prairies: the grain elevator and the oil derrick, the mine head and the factory chimney.

In every country, the land itself plays the most important part in determining the economy and the life that will unfold there. This is perhaps more true of this area than of any other place in Canada. It is the vivid, changing land of the prairies that has set the course of their history and the lives of the people who have chosen to live there.

To many people, even to some who live on the prairies, it is the feeling of empty space that is most characteristic of these provinces. There is a feeling of hollowness, of isolation and loneliness, which frightens the stranger and leaves him longing for familiar trees and hills and sounds of town. To most, however, space is one of their most precious possessions, and the feeling of aloneness gives them the knowledge that they are one with the land.

THE SEIGNIORY — II

The habitants, too, had certain duties to perform in order to remain on the land. They had to work a number of days each year, usually four, but not more than six, in the seignior's fields. In return for the use of the land, they had to make two payments a year which took the place of rent and taxes. At times these payments were made in money but more often than not, they consisted of produce such as wheat or barley or farm animals such as pigs or chickens.

At first, the seigniories were located on the major rivers and most of them extended for some distance back into the woods. The land given to the habitants was in long narrow strips, each with its own river frontage. This was the natural thing to do as the rivers were the only highways known to the settlers in the early years.

When most of the good land along the rivers was taken, a plan was devised by Jean Talon, the first Intendant, whereby the seigniories located inland were to be made circular. In the centre of the circle would be the seignior's house along with the houses of the carpenter, stonemason and shoemaker. Around this central hub would be the peasants' houses and behind the houses, the wedge-shaped plots of land. In this system the habitants were much closer together and, more important, they were close to the seignior's house in case of attack.

Despite the fact that it had been made illegal in England many years before, this feudal system of land ownership was allowed to continue even after the country came under British rule. However, as our country grew and became more industrialized, the system became outdated and it was abolished by an act of Parliament in 1854.

THE WOLF

Of the many animals that inhabit the world of nature in Canada, there is no animal about which so many lurid tales have been passed down through the centuries and that strikes more fear into the hearts of people than the wolf.

Yet, if the truth be known, imagination supplies more terror than real danger to man. This does not mean that the wolf is a pleasant little playmate; one look at its cold, yellow eyes is enough to send chills down anyone's spine. The casual forest traveller cannot be blamed either if the hairs on the nape of the neck rise when a wolf howls at the moon or runs in yelping, full cry on the hunt.

In reality, the wolf is more often heard than seen by the average person in the forests. On occasion, one may flit across the forest trail some distance ahead of the traveller or slink through the trees parallel to the path, but usually only the merest glimpse is had of this creature. Although this gives one a creepy feeling, the wolf invariably keeps a respectable distance from people.

Small brush wolves are fairly common in some wooded regions of southern Ontario, for example, and can be mistaken sometimes for wild, stray dogs. The biggest timber wolf, often up to 68 kg, roams the silent northern forests. When small game is abundant in summer, hunting is quite easy; in winter, the wolves prey on weaker deer and moose which are unable to escape them in the soft, deep snow or on the slick ice of lakes and rivers. During the winter when food is very scarce, wolves, if desperate enough, will move by night to isolated farms or communities to forage for food.

THE FORTRESS CITY — I

No city in Canada has had a more colourful and eventful history than Quebec. It is our oldest city and it is unique in that a small area of the upper town is enclosed by walls which make it the only fortified city in North America. During its long history, Quebec was considered to be so important that it served as the capital of our country on three separate occasions.

The present-day city is located on the site of the old Indian village of Stadacona which was first discovered by Cartier; however no attempt to settle the area was made until 1608, long after the village had been abandoned. The first fort, built on the river bank, was a wooden structure, two stories high, but with only three sides. There was a moat 4.5 m wide and 1.8 m deep around the fort as protection against attack.

It was more than fifteen years later, after a good road had been cut up the mountain, before construction was begun on the first of a series of permanent forts. The first one was built on the crest of Cape Diamond, more than 90 m above the river, but the fort was so poorly built that by 1629 the masonry had developed dangerous cracks and two of the corner towers had collapsed and filled the moat with rubble. It was at this opportune time that the British chose to attack. With only sixteen men and four cannon to defend it the French elected to surrender.

Quebec remained in British hands for three years before it was returned by treaty. The French then started construction on a second fort, a chateau with four towers and a balcony, 30 m below the crest of the mountain, but it was never completed. The world-famous Chateau Frontenac Hotel is located near the site of this second fort.

THE SHANTYMEN

One of the first major industries in Canada was lumbering, as not a few of the settlers found more profit in supplying the navy with timber for wooden ships than in tilling the soil. This industry expanded rapidly during the 19th century, sometimes with the tide of settlement and, at other times, ahead of it. One of the richest areas for timber was the region along the Ottawa River which divides the provinces of Ontario and Quebec.

In the early days, the shantymen, as the timber cutters of the Ottawa were called, lived and worked together in groups of thirty or forty. All through the long winter, they cut and squared the pine trees in pineries or the oaks in groves and then drew the logs by oxen to the river. When spring came, they formed the timbers into small rafts called cribs, boarded the cribs in teams, and dropped away down the rapids to the market.

During the long voyage, the men lived, ate, and slept on the cribs. Their living quarters were huts, about 1.2 m by 1.8 m, made of strips of bark, and they resembled a cylinder in shape. To these beds, or lairs, as the huts were called, were affixed trams or handles which permitted them to be carried from one place to another as the situation dictated.

Whenever the cribs came to large bodies of still water, they were brought together into one grand flotilla with masts, flags, and sails flying high. Even though sails were used, the crew often had to rely on poles or crude oars to move their large raft. It usually took these shantymen about six weeks to haul their logs down river to the market in Quebec, twelve hundred kilometres away.

The rafts and their riders vanished as steel took the place of wood in shipbuilding. The river today still carries great runs of logs, but the days of the square-timber trade are over.

THE FORTRESS CITY — II

In the years that followed, Quebec grew slowly from a simple trading post to become the social and cultural centre of New France. It was formally declared a city in 1663 even though it had a population of less than 1 000. The British tried to capture the city for a second time in 1690 but the attack was so poorly planned and executed that the French had little trouble defending the fort.

By the fateful year of 1759, the city had a population of nearly 5 000. Besides the fort, the city included a hospital, a church and monastery, a Jesuit college, the Bishop's palace and, in the lower town, the houses and stores of the people. In that year, after a siege of two months and a battle which lasted less than half a day, the British captured Quebec and with this victory France lost all its claims in the New World. The people of the city were offered free passage back to France but a good number elected to remain as their ties were with this new land, and they and their descendants have played a major role in the growth and development of our country.

The city was attacked for the last time in its history in 1775 by the Americans during their uprising against England. Quebec was under siege for five months during the long, cold winter and it was only the arrival of reinforcements in the spring that saved the city from changing hands once again.

The British rebuilt and strengthened the defences of the fort located on the crest of the mountain. The present fort, called The Citadel, is still armed today and it has often been referred to as the "Gibraltar of America." Today it is a famous tourist site and, during the summer, it serves as the residence of the Governor General of Canada.

TIMED WRITINGS 33

UPPER CANADA VILLAGE

It has only been in the past few years that we have come to appreciate what our forefathers did for us. The province of Ontario alone now has more than thirty sites devoted to preserving a part of our heritage. To many, the most complete display of the early life of Ontario is Upper Canada Village which is located on the site of the former battlefield of Chrysler Farm on the St. Lawrence River near the town of Morrisburg. During its first year of operation alone, more than a quarter million people came to see this living museum of pioneer life.

The village as such did not ever really exist. It was created by bringing together different kinds of houses and churches and furnishings that might be found in a typical house of this area and arranging them to show life as it was in the early days. Some of the houses date from an early period of settlement while others represent the prosperity and culture of a later period.

Everything in the village works. In the woollen mill, more than 100 years old, wool is processed and woven into soft blankets; giant timbers are cut in the sawmill; and crisp loaves of bread are made in an old tavern from a real pioneer recipe. There are shops where the blacksmith, cabinet-maker and weaver work at their crafts in authentic buildings. You can see women and men dressed in the costume of the day carrying out tasks that were part of the way of life of the pioneers.

There are no telephones or electric wires to be seen. The roads are dirt or made from planks and travel is by a horse-drawn cart, by ox-cart, or by bateau on the canal. Every care has been taken to preserve the atmosphere of the early days. Being there is like taking a journey into the past.

TIMED WRITINGS 44   ONTARIO

THE VOYAGEURS I

In Quebec, with its many rivers and thousands of lakes edged by dark forests, the waterways were the natural highways of war, trade, and exploration for Indians and explorers alike. Although some of the rivers have now been reduced to mere trickles, three hundred years ago they carried two or three times the volume of water that they do today.

These rivers began to dwindle with the use and abuse of the land around them by the settlers. The clearing of large areas of forest cover to make fields and farms, the draining of swamps, and poor plowing practices resulted, in time, in flash floods and soil erosion. Without the trees and swamps to act as sponges for the storage of moisture, the water escaped down the river beds far faster than the supply could replace it. As a result, brooks exist where once there were deep waters.

During the French regime, there were more than five thousand men, called voyageurs, licensed to hunt and trade for furs. Even after the land came under British rule, voyageuring continued to expand, and it more than held its own until well into the 19th century. Their usual means of transport were huge canoes made of birch bark stretched over a frame of wood. These large canoes could carry up to four tonnes of cargo, and each was propelled by a team of from six to ten paddlers. A supply of rolled bark and a quantity of gum was always carried to make the repairs that were often necessary en route.

The men who manned these canoes were a lusty, untamed breed, and it is impossible to exaggerate the colour and flavour they added to the early life of this land. Theirs was a rugged, exciting life, and those who took part in it did so with zest, usually living their lives to the fullest.

THE UNITED EMPIRE LOYALISTS — II

The story of Evangeline by the poet Longfellow, which describes the plight of the Acadians when they were deported from their homes in Nova Scotia, is well-known to many people. It is a tragic story but, as is often the case, fact can be more heart-rending than fiction. Such was the case in the story of a United Empire Loyalist named Robert Land and his family.

At the start of the American revolution, Land lived in one of the American colonies but he was a staunch Loyalist. During the conflict he was often used to carry dispatches for the British. It was while he was on one of these missions that he was shot and wounded. He managed to find a hiding place in a thicket and here he remained until he was able to continue his journey. When he finally reached home, he found it in ashes and his wife and children gone.

Land could not find any trace of his family so, broken hearted, he travelled north and settled near where the city of Stoney Creek is located today. For seven years he worked and lived alone until one night, when he returned to his cabin, he found his wife and two sons waiting for him.

The story of Mrs. Land and her two sons is equally heart-rending. They believed that he had been slain during the revolution so they fled to New Brunswick with other Loyalists. There the mother toiled until the boys reached young manhood. Then, in search of a better life, they decided to travel westward into what was then Upper Canada. When they reached Niagara they heard the story of the lonely settler called Land. Since their surname was not all that common, they wondered if this could be the long-lost husband and father. There was only one way to find out—walk the remaining 80 km through the woods. They did, and their story ended happily.

THE VOYAGEURS II

Few of the voyageurs were more than one hundred and sixty-five centimetres tall for there was little room for larger men in the canoes which were usually heavily laden with outgoing trade goods or inbound with bales of fur. They were powerful men with broad shoulders, bull necks, and muscular arms, the result of a lifetime at the paddle and the carrying of heavy loads. They could carry up to one hundred and eighty kilograms on their backs at a dog trot over the roughest portage and would paddle twelve to eighteen hours a day at forty strokes to the minute — nine kilometres per hour in calm water.

During his travels, the voyageur's days began before dawn and continued until dusk or later, and he slept rolled in a single blanket under an upturned canoe. Two meals, breakfast and supper, were the usual routine: dull fare of dried peas or cornmeal cooked in a common kettle with a small portion of pork or bacon. As there were no plates, the men hunkered around the kettle and helped themselves from it with wooden spoons.

On his journey, he dressed much as did the Indian in a red wool cap, moccasins, deerskin leggings from ankle to knees, bare thighs, breech cloth, and a gaudy sash from which hung a beaded pouch containing his pipe, tobacco, and other small necessities. To this he would add a blanket coat and, at the end of a journey or when reaching a trading post, he would deck himself in all the finery at his disposal, including large plumes for his headgear.

With the coming of roads, steam, and rails, the devil-may-care life of the voyageur faded from the scene, but for many people their spirit continues to roam the waterways of Quebec and Ontario.

THE UNITED EMPIRE LOYALISTS — I

Canada, which did not exist yet as a nation, grew slowly under English rule. The first large influx of settlers did not come from Europe as one might expect but from the United States, and it was not until the Americans had won their freedom that a mass exodus to Canada took place. The newcomers, called Loyalists by the Americans, were people who chose to remain loyal to the Crown during the war. Both during and after the conflict they suffered at the hands of former friends and neighbours. After the war was over, they were promised amnesty and restitution for the losses they had suffered. When these promises proved to be not worth the paper they were written on, as many as 50 000 Loyalists dug up their roots and came north to begin a new life.

Like the Acadians, they had to leave behind most of what they owned. In some cases their homes and their properties were taken away from them. The British government did all it could to help them but they still had to face many hardships in their new homeland. A good many of the new settlers had come from fairly wealthy homes and others had come from large towns and villages that had most of the comforts and the good things in life. Now they had only their pride and their strength.

They had to start life all over again in a land they had never seen, knew little about, and that was still, for the most part, a land of forest. They built houses, schools, churches and even roads. They carved towns and cities out of forests, many of which are now important centres, and they set up businesses which are even today of great importance to the welfare of many. They endured and they succeeded. There are families today in eastern Canada who still speak with pride as they recall what their ancestors did for a principle.

ONTARIO

Almost ninety per cent of the province of Ontario, like Quebec, is covered by a vast rocky plateau known as the Canadian Shield. For many years it was a real physical barrier to westward expansion but today it is known to harbour one of the largest treasure-houses of natural resources in the world.

The Shield, born over a billion years ago, is one of the oldest landforms of our world. Time and weather have levelled the once great mountains that made up the Shield, and the last great ice age was largely responsible for its present cold and desolate appearance. As one moves further north, one passes through an area of low, rolling hills and sharp ridges covered with heavy forest, broken only by pools and slashes of sparkling water lapping the steep walls of the cliffs. In the far north, the forest dwindles to narrow fringes of spindly trees that hug isolated patches of solid ground in swamp-like muskeg country. Much of this land is quaking bog, a paradise for wild-fowl of many kinds, almost impassable in the cool, short summer, but well marked by foot, sled and track when it is frozen in the winter.

The country south of the Shield, the remaining ten per cent of the land, is gently sloping and drains southward to the lakes and rivers that mark its southern boundary. Here may be found the most fertile earth in the province, soil left by the glacier of the last great ice age as it retreated northward some fifteen thousand years ago. The landscape is marked by low, oval hills called drumlins and by ridges of gravel-like moraine that were left behind by the glacier as it withdrew.

Although this is the smallest portion of the province in total area, it contains the major share of the population, commerce and industry.

PIONEER LIFE IN ONTARIO — II

It is difficult for us today to realize, let alone appreciate, how rigorous the life of a pioneer was. Sweat, toil, and tears was the lot of every settler, rich or poor, male or female. They had their hands and their health, but very little else. The usual first home — better ones came later with prosperity — was a simple, log shanty with dimensions of about 2.4 m by 3 m by 1.8 m. The logs were usually cut with a short-handled ship's axe, the common tool of the time, and were notched to fit each other at the corners.

The roof might be covered with thick, overlapping slabs of basswood or strips of elm bark in layers held down by tied poles. Spaces between the logs were chinked with pieces of wood and moss, then plastered inside and out with clay. Smoke from the fire on the earthen floor of the single room escaped through a hole in the roof. Many of the cabins had no windows. In those that did, settlers who could not afford glass used oiled paper or scraped skin in the window frames.

The first settlers depended upon each other much more than people do today for safety, companionship, and entertainment. A custom of that era, one that is still practised in some rural areas even today, was a community effort called a bee. Neighbours would gather from all around to build a barn, or harvest the crops if sickness had struck, or put up pickles, or even build a house for newlyweds. No matter what the occasion, if a task was too large for one family to perform, the neighbours pitched in to assist them.

Invariably, a fiddler would be present at these bees, and the settlers would wind up their work with food, dancing, and other forms of merriment. In this fashion, Ontario, the backwoods child, grew into adulthood.

THE INDIANS IN ONTARIO

The history of the white people in Canada is short in years, dating back only a few hundred years, but for untold ages before that the land was inhabited by a race of people whom the newcomers called Indians. Estimates of the number of Indians who lived in Ontario at the time the explorers first arrived vary between forty and fifty thousand, almost one-quarter of the total population of our country.

Despite the fact that there were many tribes living in the province, the Indians could be grouped into two broad classes — the hunters and the farmers. Those who lived in the dark forests of the Canadian Shield were mainly hunters as they relied on wild game and fish for most of their food and clothing. As a result, they were a migratory people who were forced to move according to the fortunes of the hunt.

The tribes that lived in the fertile land south of the Shield relied, on the other hand, on the land to provide them with much of their food; therefore, their villages tended to be of a more permanent nature. Those who lived in the south lived much as the Europeans did in their medieval, walled towns except that the walls were made of stout logs rather than mortared stone. Adjacent to the villages were the fields where crops such as corn, beans, and squash were grown.

The dwellings of the tribes that farmed the land were much larger than those of the nomadic tribes. They lived year round in huge cabins, a kind of arbor or bower covered with bark that was capable of holding up to two dozen families, possessions and all. The hunters, however, preferred smaller dome-shaped lodges which could shelter up to fifteen persons and which could be erected or dismantled very quickly.

PIONEER LIFE IN ONTARIO — I

The settlement of Ontario was very slow up until the last quarter of the 18th century, and then it began with not just a slowly rising tide, but with a solid flood of humanity surging across the land. The successful revolution of the colonies to the south was the springboard to the overnight blossoming of the land.

People who had lost their homes because they remained loyal to the Crown flocked by the tens of thousands north to the huge wilderness which later became Ontario. They were soon joined by whole regiments of soldiers who had been given grants of land as rewards for their services in the war.

Life was far from easy for these first settlers. Until the farms were developed, feed for cattle was hard to come by and staples like mutton and beef were scarce. The early settlers, like the Indians, had to depend to a large extent on fish and wild game to supply their larder. Pigs, however, which could root for their own food in the woods, were plentiful, and they were usually killed in the fall and salted down for winter provisions.

Flour was a major problem for the settlers who lived any distance from a grist mill — one of the first buildings to be constructed in a new community. Because of the great distances, many settlers were forced to use coffee grinders to produce a coarse flour called samp; others took a leaf out of the Indian's book and pounded corn in the hollowed-out stump of a tree. Maple sugar had to be used to help make the samp or cornmeal porridge more palatable. Luxuries, like tea, were difficult to obtain, and these hardy settlers made do, as they did with most things, by using the leaves of shrubs such as hemlock or sassafras.

HURONIA — I

There is a narrow strip of land in Ontario, south of the tip of Georgian Bay, that was the scene of one of the most dramatic events in the early history of our country. This land was called Huronia and at the beginning of the 17th century it was probably one of the most densely populated areas in what is now Canada. Some estimates have placed the population of the Huron nation as high as 25 000 at the time of the white settlers' arrival. The Hurons lived a very settled life, mostly farming and fishing, though they travelled widely north and west to collect furs and each year they would make the long and often difficult journey of more than 1 200 km to trade with the French at Quebec.

The story of the Huron nation has great historical importance to our country in that Champlain, in looking for a way to extend French power, chose to befriend them because they were a larger and more stable nation than the Iroquois to the south. In order to cement this new friendship, Champlain agreed to help his new allies by joining them on a raiding party against the Iroquois. In doing so he gained the friendship that he looked for but, at the same time, he gained the hatred of the Iroquois which was to have a far-reaching effect in the years that followed.

During the next three decades, the Church tried very hard to introduce their religion and way of life to the Hurons. The fathers lived and worked under difficult conditions as they were always under threat of attack by the Iroquois, so it was decided that a central residence would be built. Saint-Marie was chosen to be the model village because it was located near the centre of the Huron nation and because it had the best access to travel by water.

HURONIA — II

As well as being a place of rest for the fathers of the Church, Saint-Marie was to become a model village for the Hurons. They wanted to show their allies, by example, how they were able to live and work together in peace and harmony. By 1648, after nearly ten years of hard work, the village was completed. The village had the distinction of having the first hospital, the first school and the first social service centre in what is now Ontario. Of the total number of French who lived in Canada at that time, one-fifth of the total, sixty-six in all, lived in the village along with thousands of Hurons.

Despite the success of the village, 1648 was the beginning of the end. The Iroquois, who at first had been content with attacking canoes laden with furs, now began to invade and destroy village after village. Alone, and feeling that it was just a matter of time before they, too, would be attacked, the people moved to a small island and rather than let their model village fall into enemy hands, they burned it completely to the ground. After a cold and bitter winter on the island, during which thousands died of cold and hunger, 360 survivors made their way back to Quebec. Five of the priests who died during the attacks by the Iroquois were martyred by the Church and they are remembered today in the Martyrs' Shrine which is close by the new village of Saint-Marie.

With the death of the Huron nation, darkness fell over the area for almost 150 years. Up to the present time, the remains of only four Huron villages have been found. The most famous, Saint-Marie, has been restored to its original state and it is now open for all to see, and feel, what it would have been like living there three hundred years ago.

| 1 | 2 | 3 | 4 | 5 | 6 | 7 | 8 | 9 | 10 | 11 | 12 | 13 | 14 |